CHURCHES OF SOMERSET

PHIL DRAPER

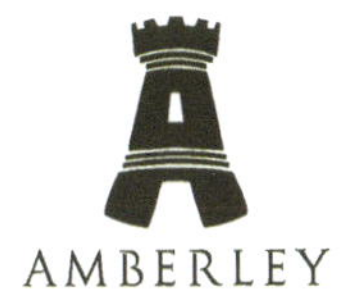

AMBERLEY

Front cover: St Mary the Virgin Church, Yatton.

Back cover: St George's Church, Hinton St George.

This edition first published 2025

Amberley Publishing
The Hill, Stroud
Gloucestershire GL5 4EP

www.amberley-books.com

Copyright © Phil Draper, 2025

The right of Phil Draper to be identified as the Author
of this work has been asserted in accordance with the
Copyrights, Designs and Patents Act 1988.

British Library Cataloguing in Publication Data.
A catalogue record for this book is available from the British Library.

ISBN 978 1 3981 2345 8 (print)
ISBN 978 1 3981 2346 5 (ebook)

Typesetting by SJmagic DESIGN SERVICES, India.
Printed in Great Britain.

Appointed GPSR EU Representative: Easy Access System Europe Oü, 16879218
Address: Mustamäe tee 50, 10621, Tallinn, Estonia
Contact Details: gpsr.requests@easproject.com, +358 40 500 3575

Contents

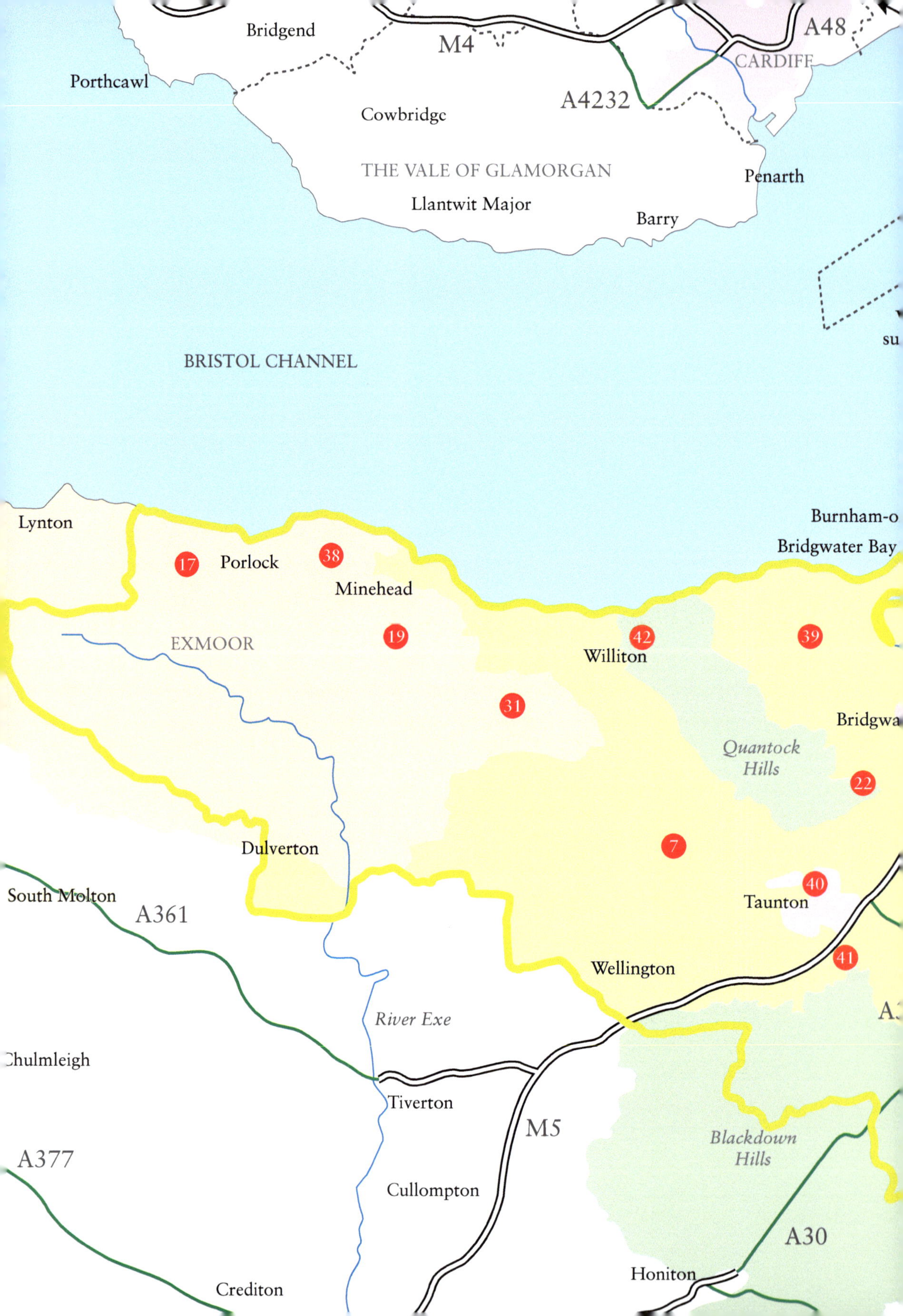

Bridgend
M4
A48
CARDIFF
Porthcawl
Cowbridge
A4232
THE VALE OF GLAMORGAN
Penarth
Llantwit Major
Barry
su
BRISTOL CHANNEL
Lynton
Burnham-o
Bridgwater Bay
17
Porlock
38
Minehead
EXMOOR
19
42
39
Williton
31
Bridgwa
Quantock
Hills
22
7
Dulverton
40
South Molton
Taunton
A361
41
Wellington
A
Chulmleigh
River Exe
A
Tiverton
M5
Blackdown
Hills
A377
Cullompton
A30
Honiton
Crediton

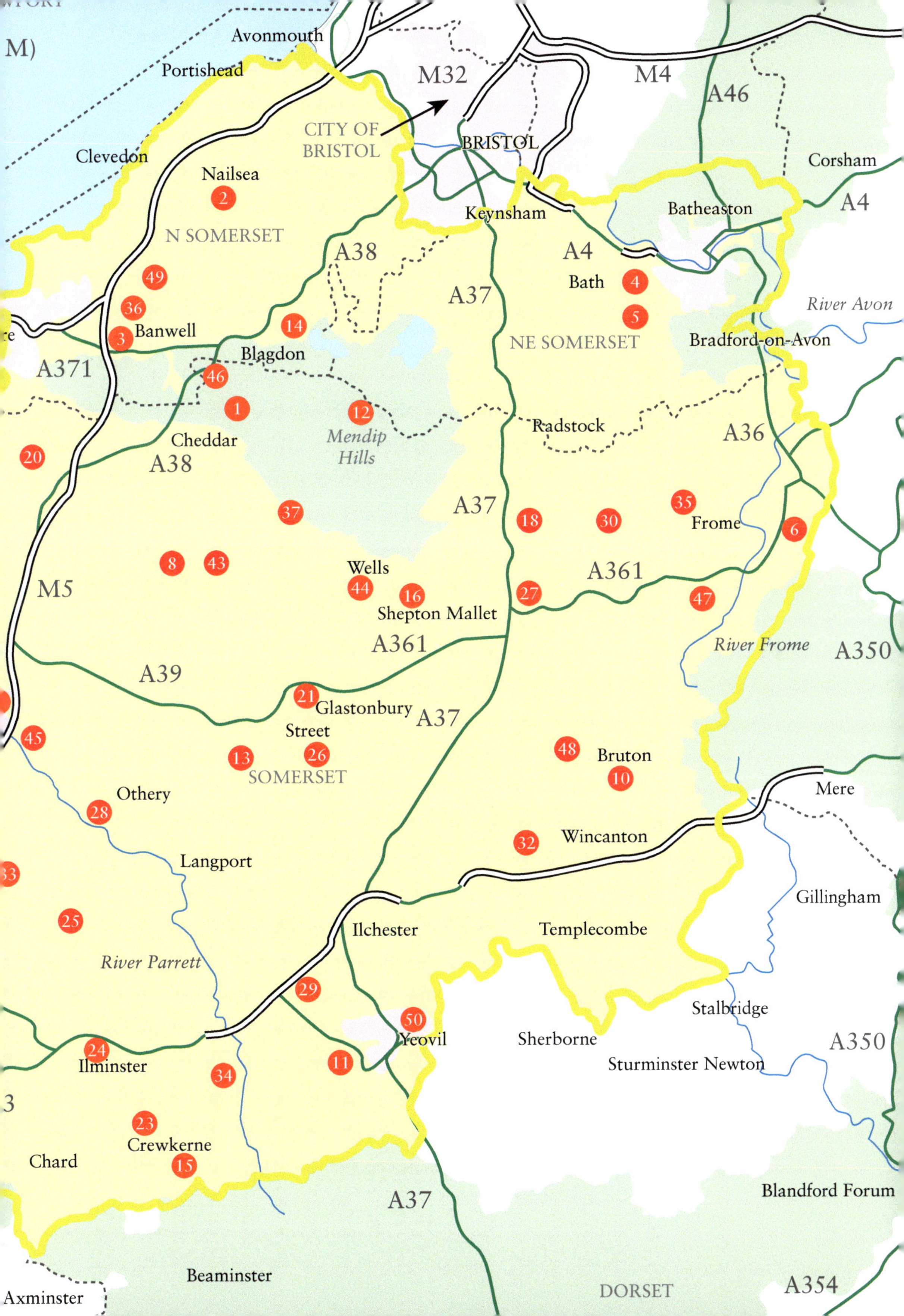

M)
Avonmouth
Portishead
M32
M4
A46
CITY OF
BRISTOL
BRISTOL
Corsham
Clevedon
Nailsea
Keynsham
Batheaston
A4
2
N SOMERSET
A38
A4
River Avon
49
A37
Bath
4
36
A38
5
Banwell
14
NE SOMERSET
Bradford-on-Avon
3
Blagdon
A371
46
A36
1
Radstock
Mendip
Cheddar
12
A37
Hills
20
A38
35
37
18
30
Frome
M5
8
43
A361
6
Wells
47
44
27
16
River Frome
A350
Shepton Mallet
A361
Street
A39
River Parrett
Langport
21
Glastonbury
A37
45
Street
48
Bruton
13
26
10
Mere
SOMERSET
Othery
28
32
Wincanton
Gillingham
Langport
25
Ilchester
Templecombe
Stalbridge
33
29
50
A350
24
Yeovil
Sherborne
Ilminster
11
Sturminster Newton
34
3
23
Crewkerne
Chard
15
Blandford Forum
Axminster
Beaminster
DORSET
A354

KEY

1. Axbridge, St John the Baptist
2. Backwell, St Andrew
3. Banwell, St Andrew
4. Bath, St Michael Without
5. Bath, Prior Park Chapel
6. Berkley, St Mary the Virgin
7. Bishops Lydeard, St Mary
8. Blackford, Holy Trinity
9. Bridgwater, St Mary
10. Bruton, St Mary
11. Brympton d'Evercy, St Andrew
12. Cameley, St James
13. Compton Dundon, St Andrew
14. Compton Martin, St Michael and All Angels
15. Crewkerne, St Bartholomew
16. Croscombe, St Mary
17. Culbone, St Beuno
18. Downside Abbey, St Gregory the Great
19. Dunster, St George
20. East Brent, St Mary the Virgin
21. Glastonbury, St John the Baptist
22. Goathurst, St Edward
23. Hinton St George, St George
24. Ilminster, St Mary the Virgin
25. Isle Abbots, St Mary the Virgin

26. Kingweston, All Saints
27. Leigh-on-Mendip, St Giles
28. Low Ham, Dedication Unknown
29. Martock, All Saints
30. Mells, St Andrew
31. Nettlecombe, St Mary
32. North Cadbury, St Michael
33. North Curry, St Peter and St Paul
34. Norton-sub-Hamdon, St Mary
35. Orchardleigh, St Mary
36. Puxton, Holy Saviour
37. Rodney Stoke, St Leonard
38. Selworthy, All Saints
39. Stogursey, St Andrew
40. Taunton, St Mary Magdalen
41. Trull, All Saints
42. Watchet, St Decuman
43. Wedmore, St Mary
44. Wells, St Cuthbert
45. Westonzoyland, St Mary the Virgin
46. Winscombe, St James the Great
47. Witham Friary, Blessed Virgin Mary, St John the Baptist and All Saints
48. Wyke Champflower, Holy Trinity
49. Yatton, St Mary the Virgin
50. Yeovil, St John the Baptist

Introduction

The landscape of Somerset is very varied, from the wild upland of Exmoor, the lowland of the Levels, the coastal resorts of the Bristol Channel, and the hills of the Quantocks, Blackdowns and Mendips. This book concerns the historic county which is today divided into three unitary authorities, Somerset, North Somerset and Bath & North-East Somerset, the two latter council areas once part of the short-lived county of Avon. The settlements are varied, from the large conurbations of Taunton, Yeovil, Weston-super-Mare, Frome and Bath to small villages with little more than a few farms and cottages, plus of course England's smallest city, Wells, with its charming medieval core surrounding the mighty cathedral. Wells is the ecclesiastical capital of Somerset, but in medieval times was rivalled by the great abbey at Glastonbury only 6 miles away which is now in ruins. The seaside resorts – Portishead, Clevedon, Weston-super-Mare, Burnham, Minehead and Porlock – all grew up around medieval churches and received additional churches in Victorian times, as did Frome, and the expanding city of Bath has incorporated several medieval villages in its suburbs as well as building new churches.

My records show that there are some 640 churches in the county and the challenge for me has been to select just fifty of these for inclusion in this book. My choice has been made to reflect different periods, styles and locations and to introduce others that are little known. To achieve this some of the churches in Somerset that may be expected to be included will be found to be missing by the reader. References to some of these other omitted churches are included in the descriptions that follow. The cathedral at Wells and the abbey church in Bath are also not included. Personally, I find every church to be of interest and because one does not appear in this book mustn't be taken to mean that you shouldn't visit. There can often be something unexpected inside.

Many of the churches are open during the day; those in towns and closer to Bristol may present more of a challenge to access. If the church is locked, hopefully you will find a notice of where to find the key on the church noticeboard.

A special mention must be made about the impressive collection of towers in the county, dating mainly from the fourteenth to sixteenth centuries, many included in this book. Some of the most spectacular are attached to more humble buildings which makes you question why so much money was spent on the tower and not on rebuilding the church itself. There must also have been some sense of competition with neighbouring parishes in medieval times! Several superb towers are not included in this book, so special mention must be made of Chewton Mendip, Dundry, Huish Episcopi, North Petherton and Wrington, which are all most memorable. Another feature is the medieval woodwork and carpentry to be found in the county, from roofs (such as Martock, Shepton Mallet and Somerton) to screens (as at Minehead, Dunster and Carhampton to name but a few) and bench ends. Many examples of the latter can be found in churches in the Quantocks.

I have been helped immensely by being able to refer to a copy of William Newsom's photographic archive of the churches in the diocese of Bath & Wells. He had been in many of the churches more recently than I had and photographed some details and items that I had missed during my visits. Two of his photographs appear in this book (Bridgwater and Selworthy) and are used with his kind permission. The rest of the photographs are my own. I am also indebted to Charmian Adams who read through my text and raised many sensible suggestions to correct or explain further what I had written.

1. AXBRIDGE, ST JOHN THE BAPTIST

This small market town at the foot of the Mendip Hills has greatly benefitted from the building of a bypass on the site of the former railway ('Strawberry Line') from Yatton to Cheddar and Wells. The church is raised above the Square and reached by a series of steps. It was rebuilt in the later fourteenth and fifteenth centuries and has large Perpendicular windows. All is grouped around a tall central tower with a pierced parapet. There are also pierced parapets to the aisles and chapels but that of the porch is Victorian. They were a later embellishment as witnessed by the way they interrupt the west gable of the nave. An unusual feature is the west porch with a small two-storey extension on the south side. The main entrance is via the south porch which has a panelled ribbed stone ceiling. Immediately you see the elaborate plastered nave roof, painted blue, and dated 1636, made by a local plasterer George Drayton who was paid a grand total of 10 guineas (£10.50p) for his work. The ribs are picked out in white and there are large pendant bosses at the apex. There was a similar roof in the chancel, but this was removed during J. D. Sedding's careful restoration in the late 1870s. Sedding then embarked on designing a complete set of fittings, choir stalls, pulpit, benches with Perpendicular traceried ends and the notable parclose screens in the chancel. These screens owe much to the Arts & Crafts movement and have carved panels in the doors with pretty hedgerow fruits and animals. Older is the fifteenth-century font with panelled shafted stem and a bowl decorated with quatrefoils. Under the bowl are some very fine shield-bearing angels; apparently, they were plastered over, perhaps to save it from damage during the Commonwealth, and only rediscovered when someone idly picked off a bit of plaster during the nineteenth century. Also of note is the collection of monuments, the oldest being the brasses in the north transept with kneeling figures of Roger Harper (d. 1493) and his wife. Anna Prowse (d. 1668) kneels stiffly under a shallow arch with a big architectural surround at the east end of the south chapel. The colours have been restored and the flanking mermaids are rather fun. In the same position in the north chapel is William Prowse (d. 1670), a very different affair, his three-quarter figure faces out from

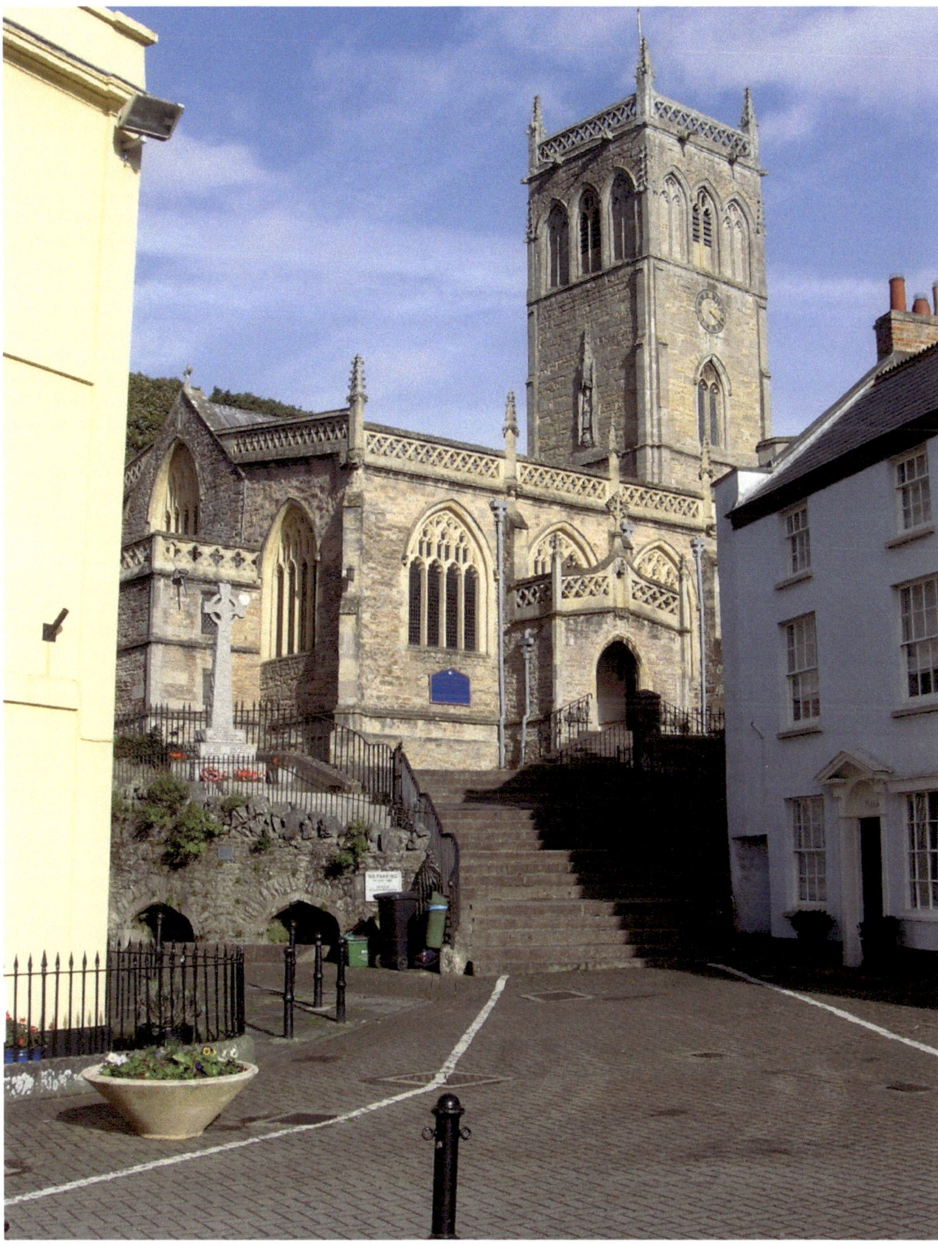

Axbridge. Looking up from the Square. Note how the aisle parapets interrupt the gable of the nave.

an oval niche in the centre of a black and white architectural framework. In a cabinet at the east end of the north aisle is an embroidered altar frontal made in the early eighteenth century by Abigail Prowse, daughter of Dr George Hooper, Bishop of Bath & Wells, showing how a Communion table was arranged. It took

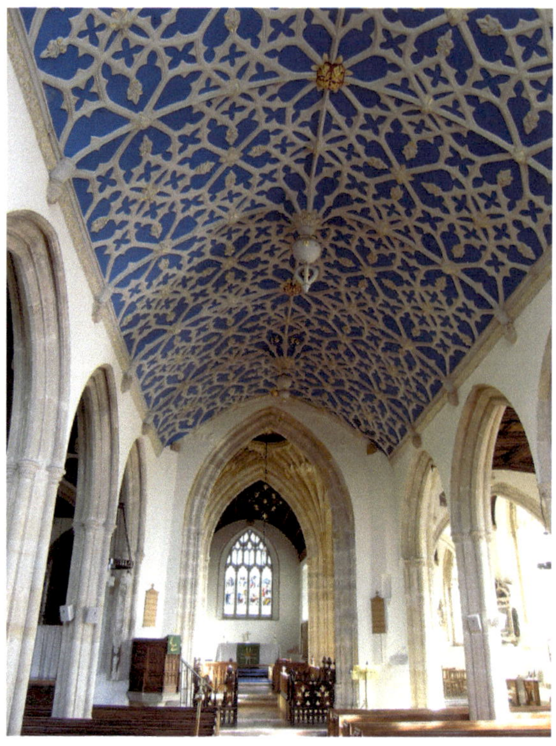

Axbridge. Interior showing the elaborate plastered nave roof, dated 1636, by George Drayton.

her nearly ten years to complete. By the south door on your way out you will see a cupboard containing symbolic loaves, part of William Spearing's (d. 1690) bequest to the poor of the town. Under this bequest, bread is still distributed today, over 300 years later.

2. BACKWELL, ST ANDREW

Backwell is a large dormitory village on the A370 Weston to Bristol road. Many people driving through will miss the medieval parish church which is set in quieter surrounds away from the busy centre and reached by turning south at the traffic lights at the crossroads. From the outside the church appears to be mainly fifteenth-century Perpendicular, apart from the impressive entrance to the south porch of *c.* 1300. Later, maybe the top of the tower and of course the modern parish hall and rooms which were added in the 1980s on the north side of the church. The tower is over 100 feet (30m) high, three stages of fairly standard Somerset design, but the top stage is decidedly odd thanks to an ogee gable moulding above the twin bell openings which is carried through the pierced parapet to finish in a small finial; large crocketed corner pinnacles are set diagonally each with four sub-pinnacles, the north-east pinnacle over the stairs taller and with a spirelet as per local fashion (a 'Bristol spirelet'). Inside the tower cuts into the Decorated Gothic arcades which have slim octagonal columns. The aisles march one bay further east of the chancel arch to form side chapels, all three separated from the nave by early sixteenth-century wooden screens. The north side of the chancel is complicated to understand. A low arch from the aisle leads into a chantry chapel, vaulted with close-set cusped transverse ribs dating from the early sixteenth century. However, the arch towards the chancel, also cusped, is fourteenth-century work. This is better appreciated from the chancel side where an ogee arch continues up into a luxuriously carved finial flanked by impressive pinnacles, similar to those seen in Bristol cathedral. Any fourteenth-century monument that was here has gone; the present tomb chest and effigy of Sir Walter Rodney (d. 1466) now stands here. Behind is a stone screen, with doorway, which was inserted in the early sixteenth

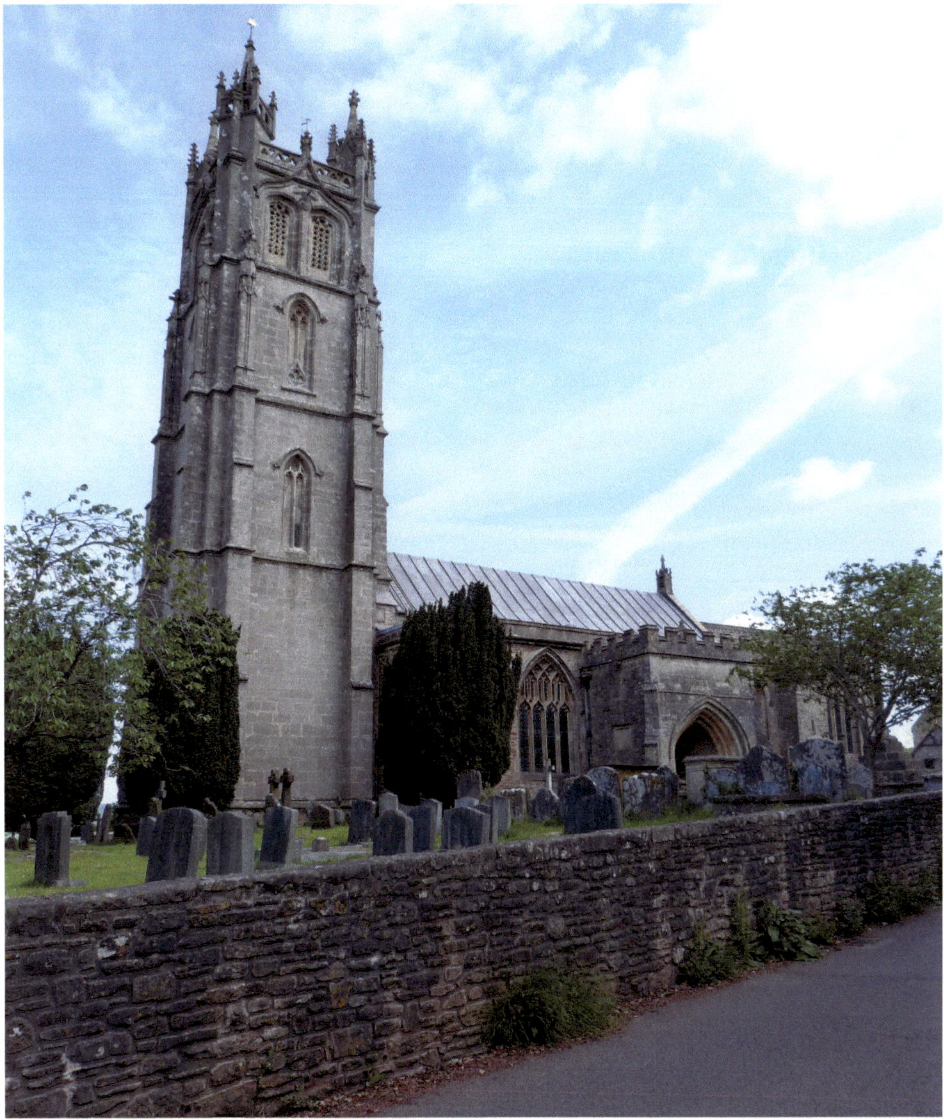

Backwell. The exterior from the south-west. Note the odd top stage of the tower.

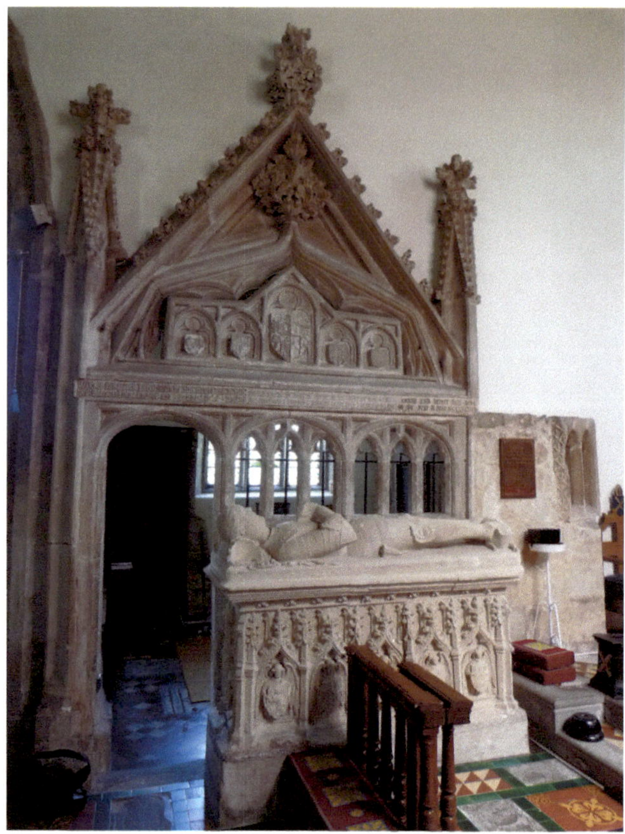

Backwell. The tomb chest and effigy of Sir Walter Rodney (d. 1466) in front of the later screen.

century and the arch filled with an inscription commemorating Elizabeth Rodney (d. 1536) who created this chapel. In the chapel, don't miss the monument to Rice Davis (d. 1636): three brass plates with incised kneeling figures in a stone surround flanked by amusing bare-breasted ladies. In the north-east corner is a two-storeyed vestry. Also of note is the brass chandelier of 1786 and the Norman font with cable moulding around the bowl and a band of foliage at the base.

3. BANWELL, ST ANDREW

This large village, its narrow roads often choked with traffic, is soon to benefit from a bypass. The church stands in the centre, reached by a short street with the 100-foot (30m) four-staged west tower at the end. Above the west window is a tableau of the Annunciation, the blank window contains a lily vase, and the figures of Mary and Gabriel are in the flanking niches. The church was rebuilt between the late fourteenth and early fifteenth centuries and there are pierced parapets with cusped triangles over all but the chancel. The clerestory may have been a late change in plan – see the figure of St Andrew on the tower just below the nave roof which would originally have been outside. Note the unusual moulding around the clerestory windows with trefoil heads, further embellished by timber tracery in the spandrels; above each window is an angel with outstretched wings. There are plenty of bosses too in the nave's wagon roof. The very fine rood screen dates from *c.* 1520, its gilding renewed in 1865 but based on the original painting of 1524. The font is Norman, the bowl carved in the later fifteenth century with upright plants and band of quatrefoils. The stone pulpit is Perpendicular and similar to

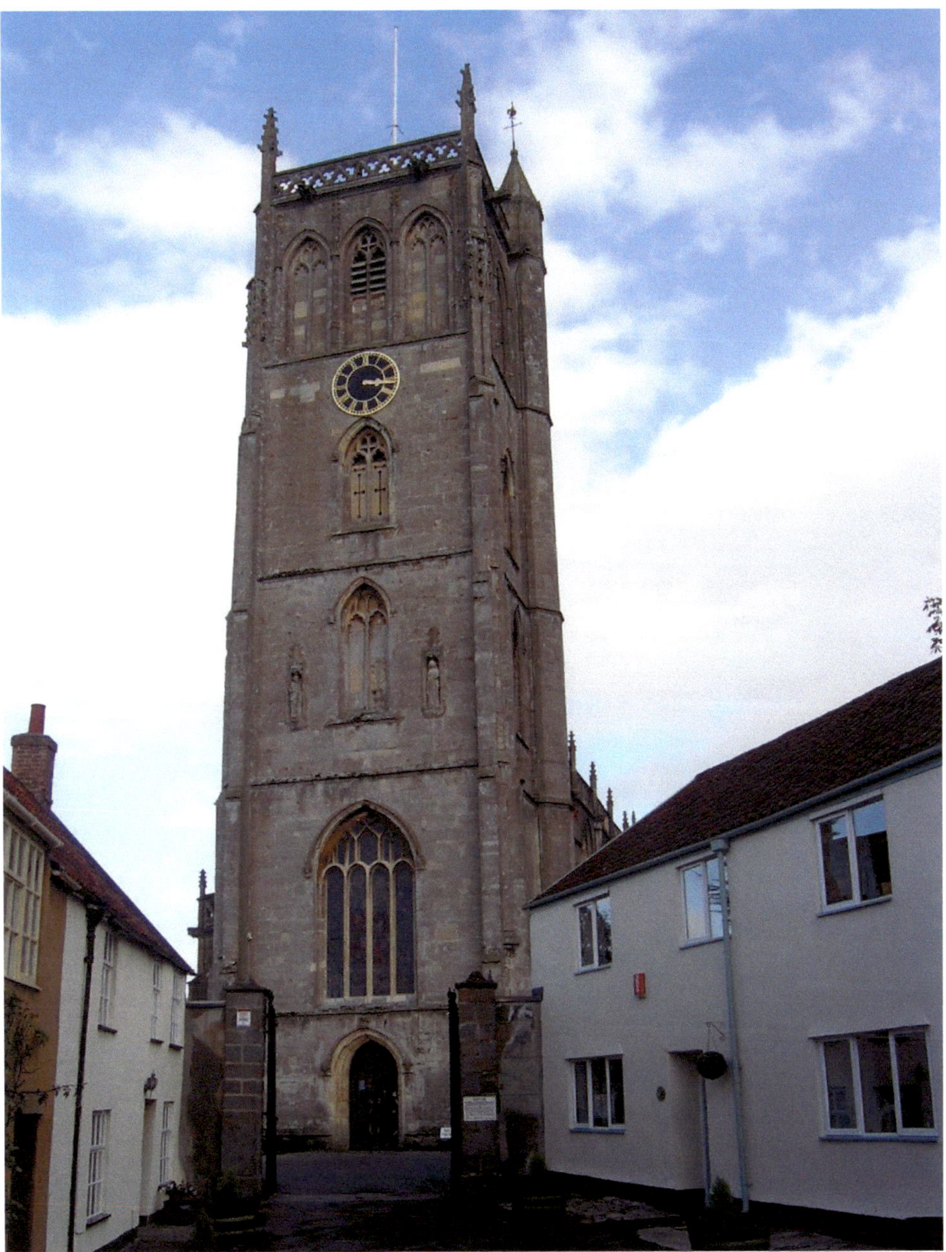

Banwell. The west tower. The tableau of the Annunciation is above the window.

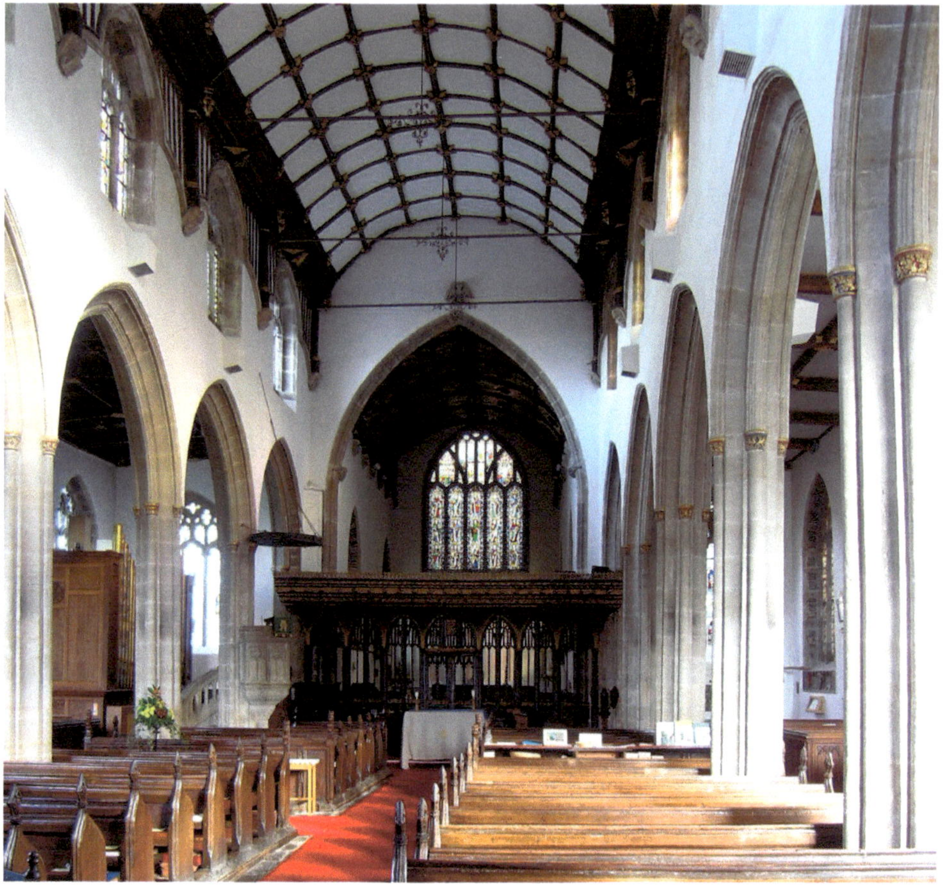

Banwell. The interior looking east showing the fine rood screen.

others found in this part of North Somerset. The sounding board is dated 1620 and the staircase was added in 1884. Monuments are few, chief among them three brasses of the fifteenth and sixteenth centuries.

4. BATH, ST MICHAEL WITHOUT

Standing to the north of the abbey church, St Michael's Church is built on a medieval site, originally standing outside of the city walls – hence its name, which differentiates it from another church called St Michael Within. It was rebuilt in 1732–42, and again 1834–37 by the local architect G. P. Manners, who worked in the city for nearly forty years. This is his best church, the triangular site between Broad Street and Walcot Street showing off the impressive steeple at its best when viewed from Northgate Street. The side walls are quite ornate with windows of three-stepped lancets and, above, a frieze of arches and a parapet of blank arcading. The fifth bay on the (ritual) south side is treated like a transept with several gables and larger pinnacles. Each bay is divided by a buttress carrying a

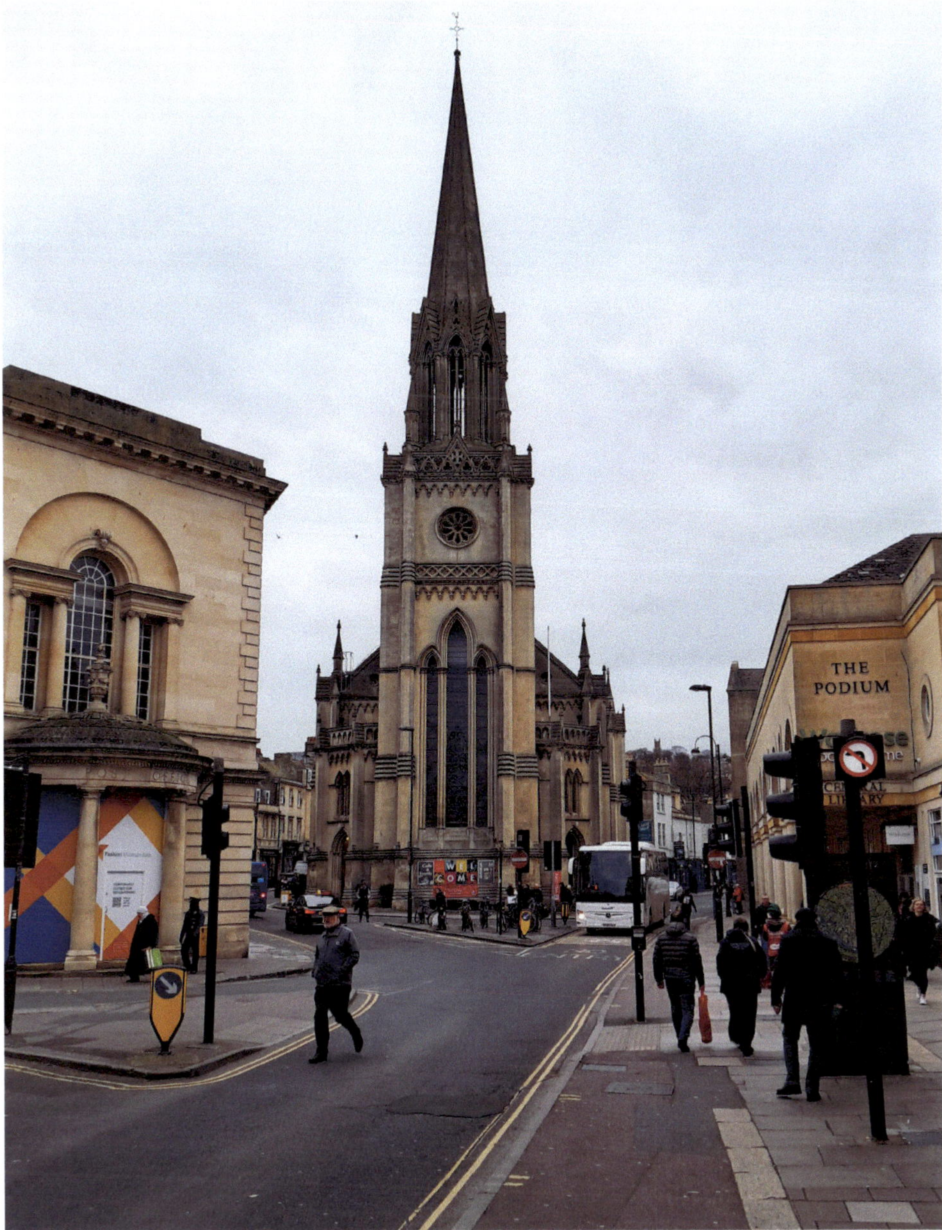

Bath, St Michael. From Northgate Street showing the 'architectural trick' west window.

pinnacle. Polygonal porches flanking the tower have internal stairs to the galleries. The Gothic interior has nave and aisles of the same height with slim pillars supporting plaster vaulting and a shallow east apse. Galleries in the aisles were removed in 1899 and the interior reordered 2005–06 when the wood and glass bridge was built across the tower arch. Interestingly, outside, the tower has a tall

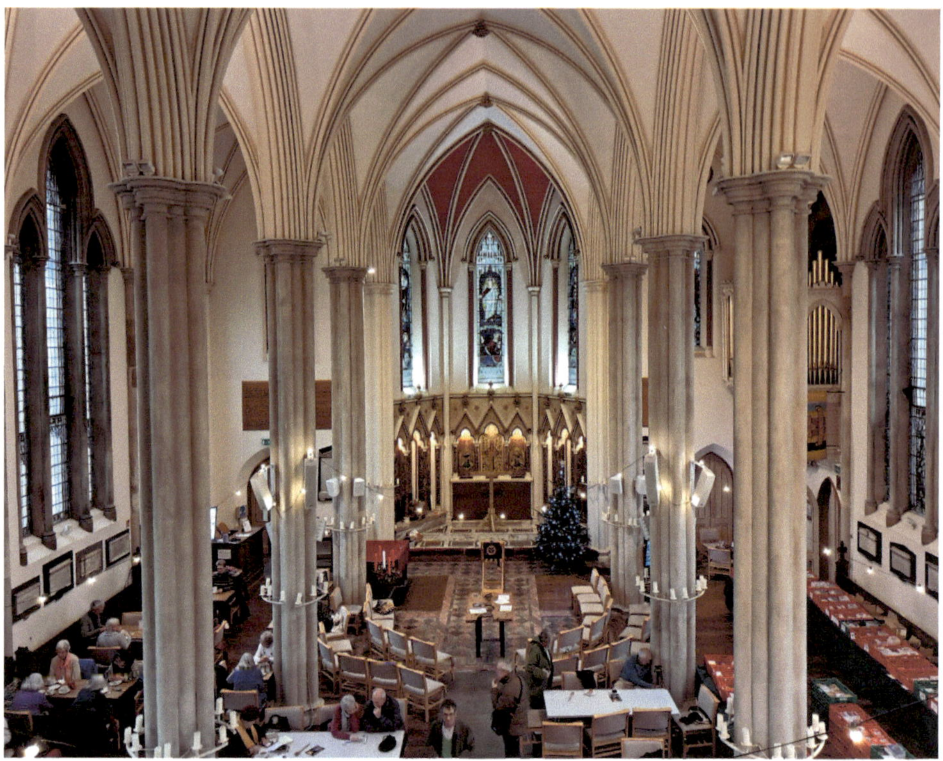

Bath, St Michael. Interior looking towards the apse from the gallery.

stepped three light window of impressive height, but this is an architectural trick as if you look carefully only the lower half of the middle light has stained glass and this is the only section that you see inside. The café created under the tower is popular with city workers and visitors alike.

5. BATH, PRIOR PARK CHAPEL

Prior Park started out as a classical Palladian mansion built 1734–43 for postmaster Ralph Allen at the head of a landscaped valley. It was constructed to show off the Bath stone from the quarries he had acquired and from which he made his fortune. In 1828 it was purchased by Bishop Baines to become a Roman Catholic college and a seminary. Following insolvency, the main house became a grammar school, which changed to a public school in 1924. The large chapel was begun in 1844, designed by J. J. Scoles and completed by his son A. J. Scoles but not until 1882. It adjoins the west wing of the college and is connected to the main house by a curved corridor. Ten bays long, the massive side walls have pedimented windows and blind panels above. A clerestory is recessed behind the parapets and the church terminates in a bold apse. On the road side, the first and the tenth bays of the lowest elevation are vermiculated and rusticated and between the two is a later cloister. Above the first bay there

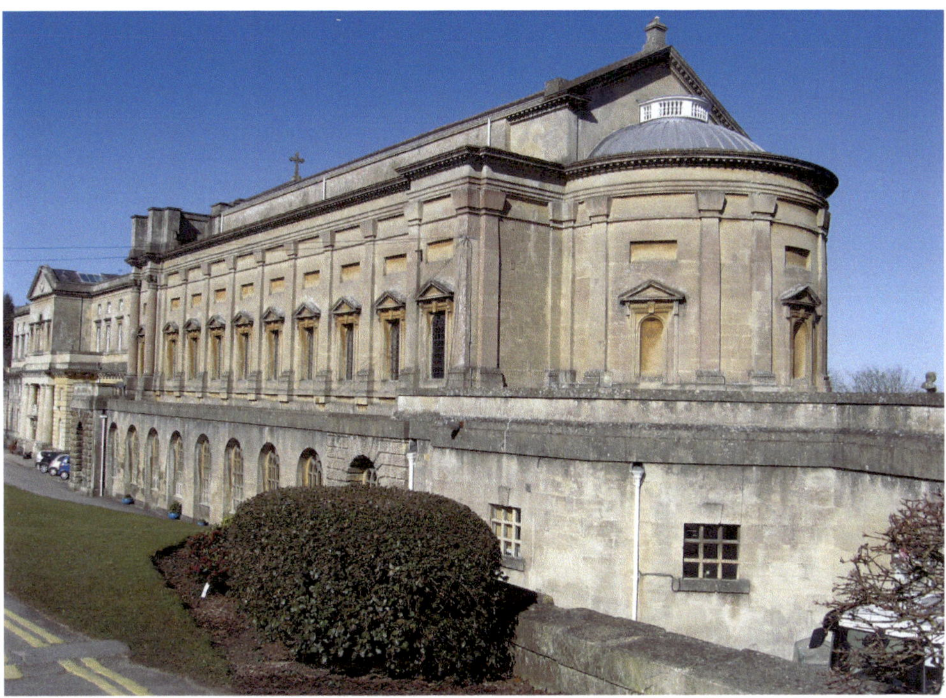

Bath, Prior Park Chapel. Note the uncarved capitals of the pilasters.

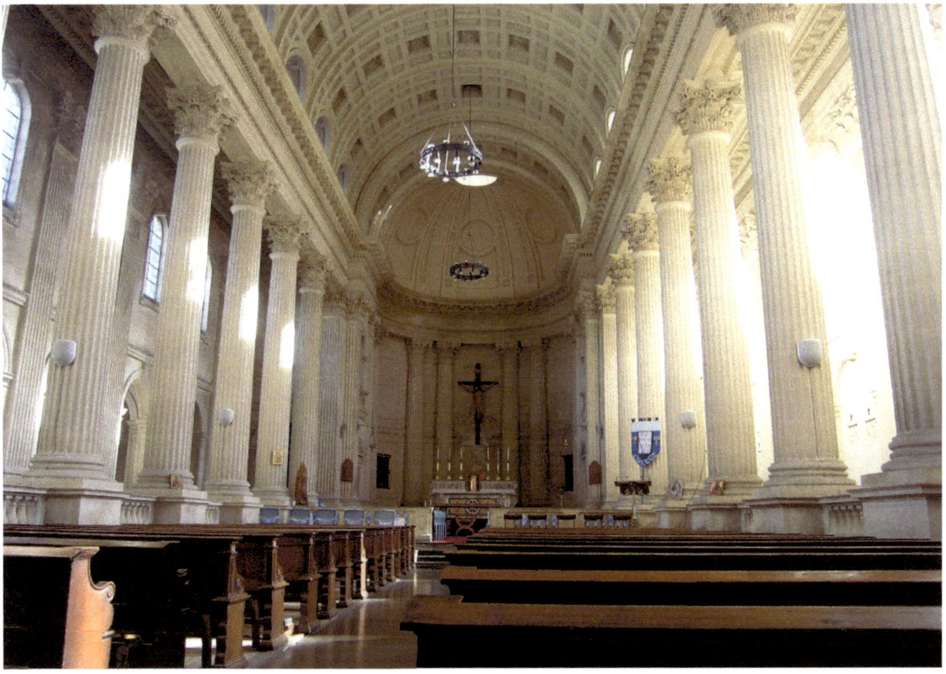

Bath, Prior Park Chapel. The breathtaking interior looking east.

are Corinthian columns, but the rest here and around the apse have been left uncarved. Not so inside; giant fluted Corinthian columns support an entablature and coffered tunnel-vault. There are similar ornate Corinthian pilasters in the aisle outer walls and around the apse. The whole is breathtaking. Sadly, the chapel is not usually open to the public but arrangements can be made to visit by contacting the school (01225 835353). The landscaped grounds to the north are now the property of the National Trust.

6. BERKLEY, ST MARY THE VIRGIN

The owner of Berkley House, Thomas Prowse, was an amateur architect and it is likely that he designed this church, rebuilt in 1750–51 on the site of its medieval predecessor. A long tree-lined path leads to the west tower, which doubles as a porch. The top of the tower is a little awkward, an over-wide cornice and a recessed balustrade above with tall vases at the corners. The rest of the exterior is rather plain but on entering the architect can be forgiven; the interior is a square with four Ionic columns supporting a central square over which is a beautiful octagonal domed roof with lantern, painted Wedgwood blue and with fine stucco

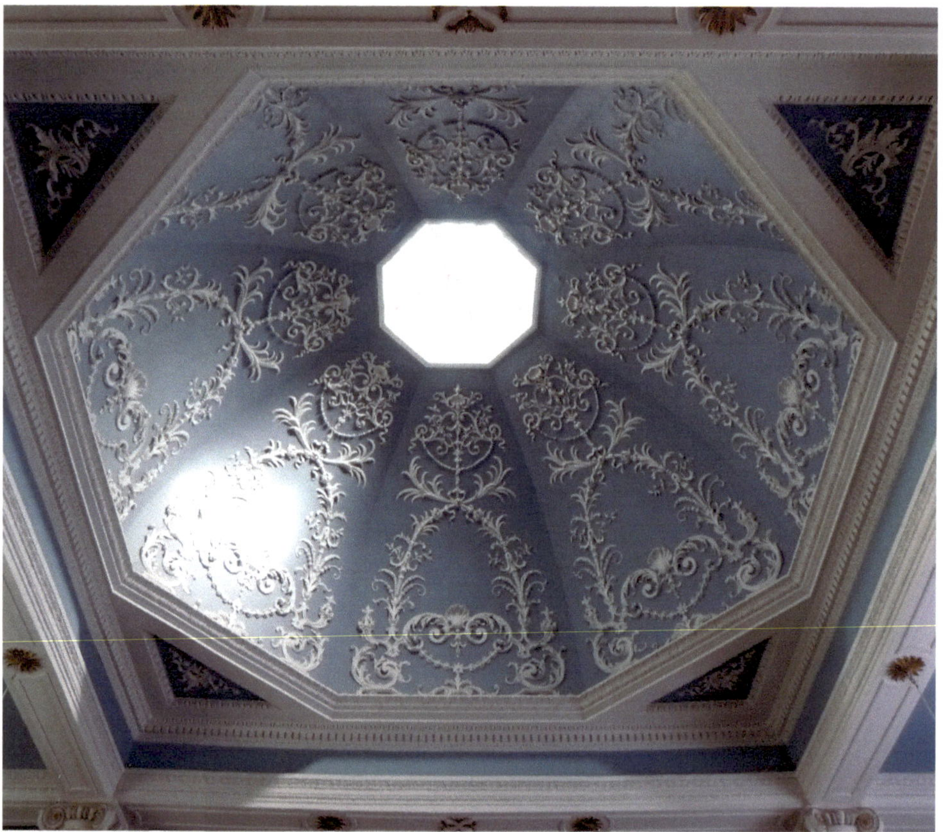

Berkley. The octagonal domed roof painted Wedgwood blue.

decoration. There is a shallow tunnel-vaulted recess for the altar, with a rather unfortunate triple-arched window of *c.* 1870, neo-Norman with heavy detailing. There is an equally brutal stone pulpit.

7. BISHOPS LYDEARD, ST MARY

The church has one of Somerset's great towers, dating from around 1500. It is technically of four stages but is really five, as the lowest part is the equivalent height of two of the others. The red sandstone exterior is shown off to its advantage by the large churchyard. The church itself predates the tower and is a product of several phases of work. The arcades are of different heights, that on the north is earlier and lower than the other but was remodelled to match. There is much medieval woodwork, the nave roof and bosses with a ceilure, bench ends (sixteenth century, of various designs mainly tracery and spindly plants but also a windmill, a green man, a pelican, a hare, a stag, rabbits, a sailing ship and the Five

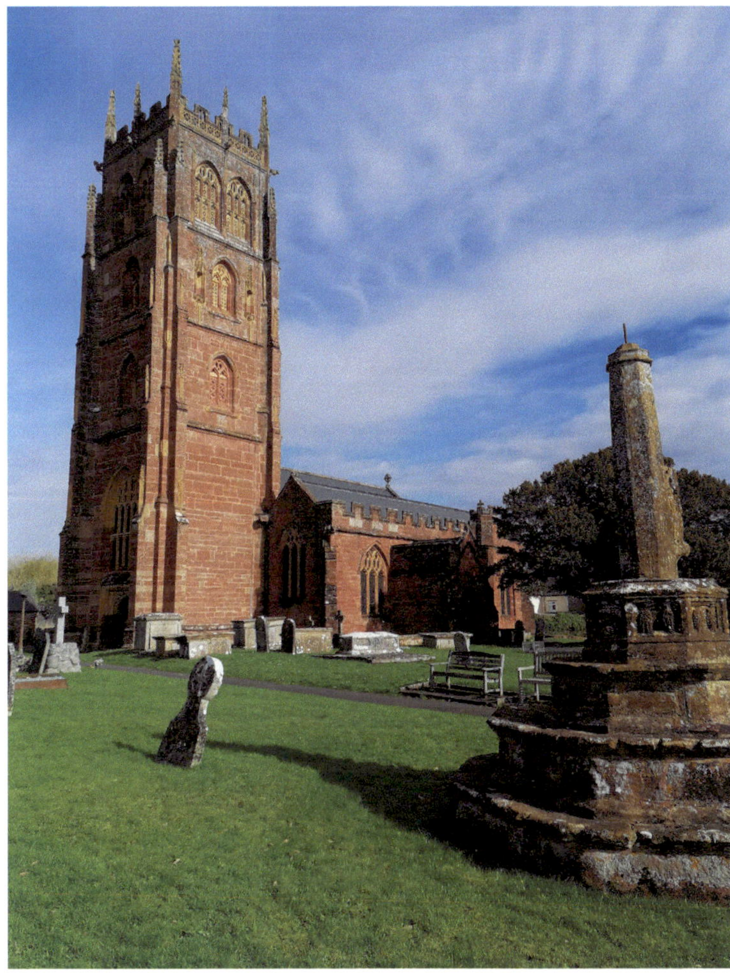

Bishops Lydeard. The impressive tower and the fifteenth-century churchyard cross.

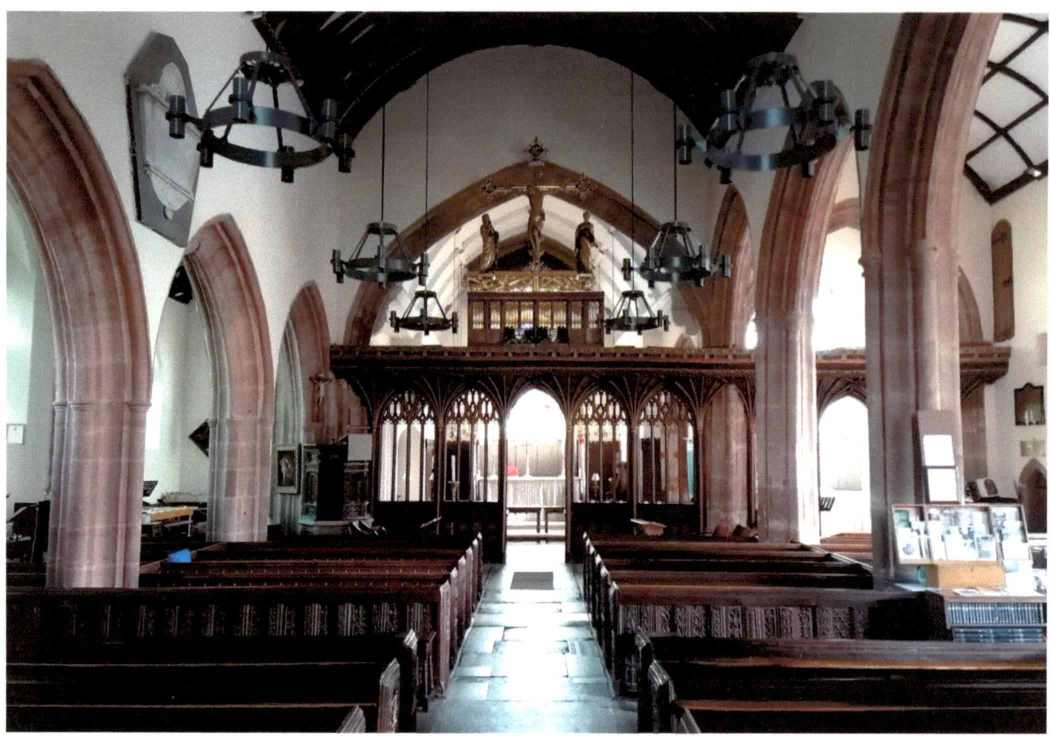

Bishops Lydeard. The interior looking east showing the fine screen with its replacement rood figures by Comper.

Wounds of Jesus) and the fine rood screen (also sixteenth century) across the nave and south aisle. All of these, together with the Jacobean pulpit, were coloured from 1923 by Sir Ninian Comper. By him, too, are the golden canopy over the altar, the matching painted splays of the east window and the gilded angels atop riddel posts in the sanctuary. He also added the rood figures in 1948. In the south aisle is a fine incised brass panel to Nicholas Grobham (d. 1585) and wife Eleanor. The couple are shown kneeling either side of a prayer desk with an elaborate sunburst with dove above, the three sons and two daughters kneel behind their parents. Don't miss the cherub blowing bubbles in the top left-hand corner. Outside there are two medieval crosses. The churchyard cross has an octagonal base with worn panels showing the Apostles in pairs and two depictions of Christ. On the shaft is a canopied niche with a figure of St John the Baptist. The market cross, removed to the churchyard in the nineteenth century, is less well preserved.

8. BLACKFORD, HOLY TRINITY

Somerset has two Blackfords; this one is near Wedmore, of which it was a chapel of ease until 1844. The church was built 1821–23 to the designs of Richard Carver, county surveyor, who was responsible for many other churches in the area. Most of his churches are fairly pedestrian, but Holy Trinity is among his best work.

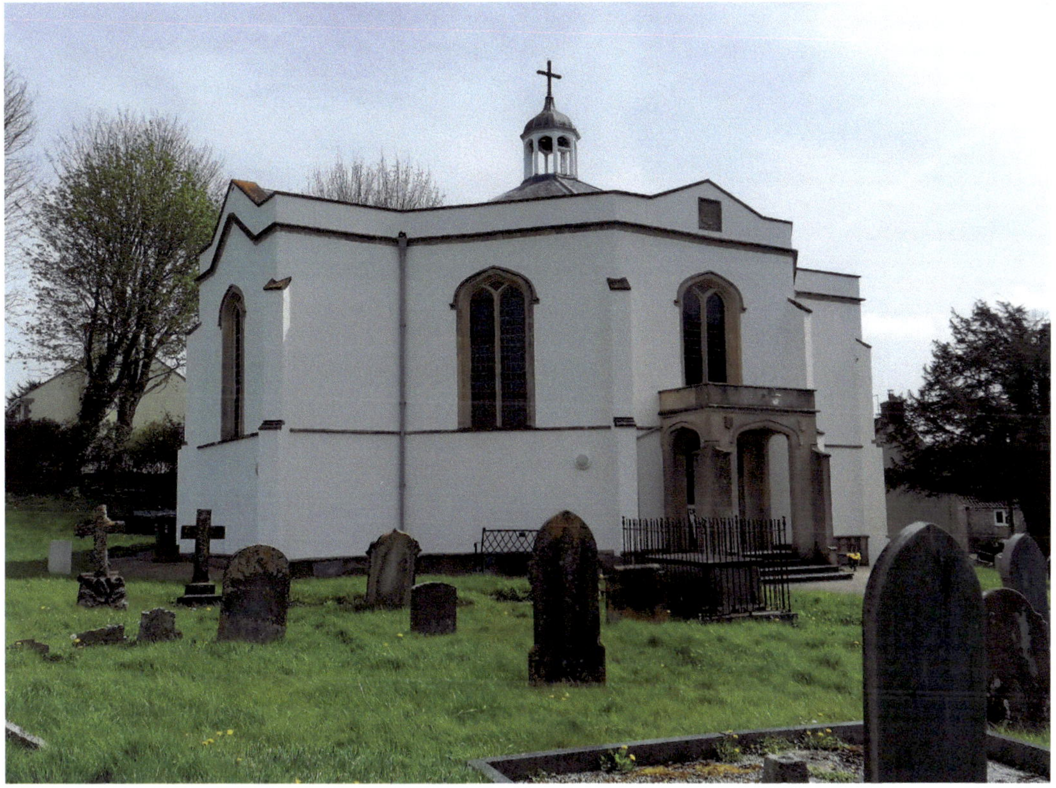

Blackford. This unusual polygonal church has recently been whitened.

It is octagonal in plan with projecting wings at the cardinal points, although that at the west end is merely a porch. By the 1890s the church was in need of repair and the parish took the opportunity to replace all the seating which had been described in the local press as 'causing great discomfort to all who attended'. The galleries were removed from the transepts and new fittings installed, completed in 1895. Further work, including rebuilding the chancel, took place in 1914, and more recently in 2006 (new vestry, toilet and kitchen area) and 2014 when the organ was removed from the west gallery to the south transept. The west gallery is the only surviving fitting by Carver. His other chapel of ease for the Wedmore parish also survives at Theale where Christ Church was built 1826–28 which was also assigned a parish in the same year as Blackford.

9. BRIDGWATER, ST MARY

This large medieval church owes much of its appearance today to the architect William Hayward Brakspear of Manchester who worked here in 1849–54. He added the clerestory, replaced the battlemented parapets with the pierced ones throughout and renewed much of the window tracery. The plain tower dates from around 1300, embattled with large stepped diagonal buttresses and with a taller square embattled turret over the stairs. The spire is one of Somerset's rare features, shear and slender, reaching 187 feet (57m) high and visible from afar. The north aisle has an impressive doorway of unusual design. The main arch seems to be of *c.* 1300 with small heads supporting the inner order but later a second arch with leaf scroll decoration and two heads was inserted and the space above filled by tracery; the two niches above are Brakspear's. The impressive interior is also largely Brakspear's design; he removed galleries and pews of varying heights and, along with the clerestory, provided new roofs, that in the nave a particularly satisfying hammerbeam construction. The nave arcades are of six bays, the eastern one slightly taller and wider for the transepts. The fussy chancel roof is also his but does incorporate some medieval bosses. He moved the prominently sited Jacobean Corporation's pew to the south transept where it now forms a long screen. The carved detail is truly spectacular; at the base of each column is a face and at the top a complete seated figure breaking up the frieze with a multitude of fantastical men, beasts, angels and birds as well as the legend 'Fear God. Honour the King.' Brakspear's too is the east window of the chancel, only visible outside as it is hidden inside by a large Italian painting, *The Descent from the Cross*, dating from

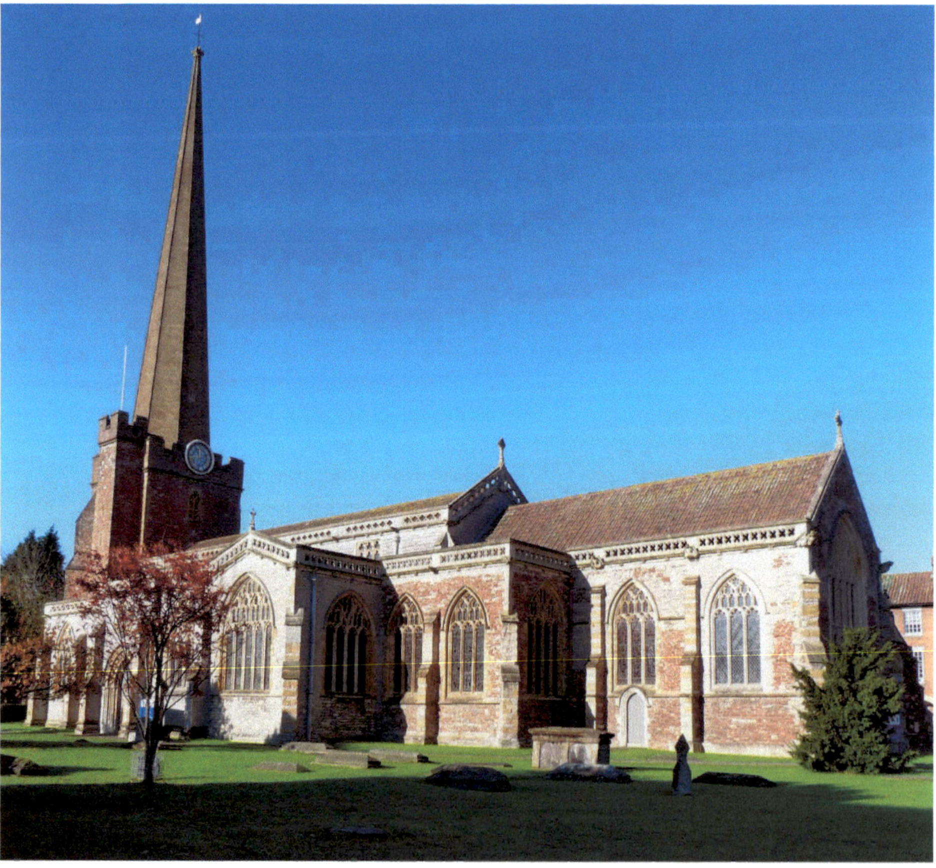

Bridgwater, St Mary. The exterior from the south-west showing the disproportionately tall spire.

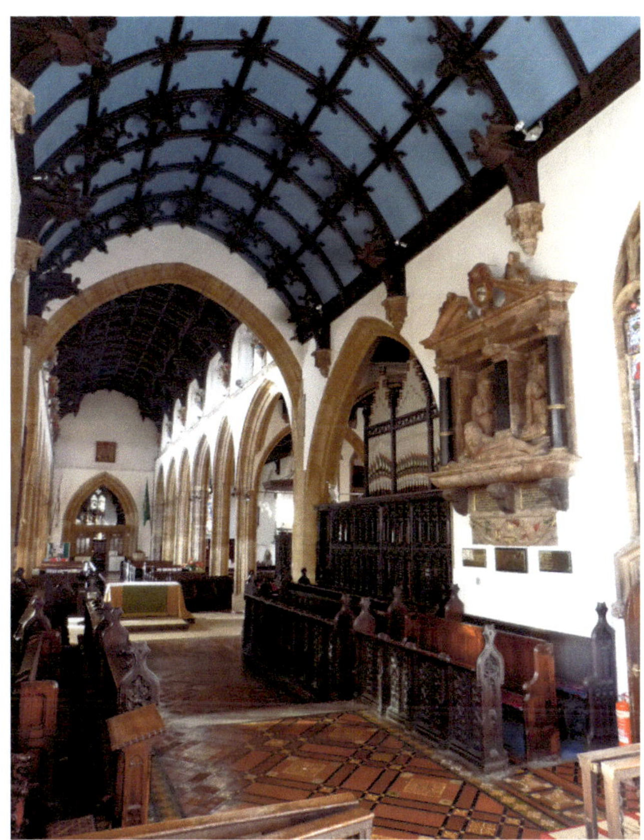

Bridgwater, St Mary. The interior looking west showing the monument to Sir Frances Kingsmill (d. 1620). (Photo by William Newsom)

around 1700, which hangs here. Apparently, this was taken from a Spanish ship as a prize and given to the church by local Member of Parliament Anne Poulett (a man, named after his godmother Queen Anne) in 1780. Brakspear hoped that the painting would be re-sited. Also in the chancel is a fine wall monument of Watchet alabaster to Sir Frances Kingsmill (d. 1620) with him semi-reclining in front of his two kneeling sons, and an octagonal table with openwork tracery dating from the fifteenth century and thought to have been originally a hanging pyx (or tabernacle for the Blessed Sacrament) and thus a very rare survival. Wells Cathedral has an earlier fourteenth-century example. In the nave is a very finely carved fifteenth-century wooden pulpit on a stone base. The upper rooms of the porches open into the church but it is not known if this an original feature or a Brakspear invention, but it is quite unique.

10. BRUTON, ST MARY

This large proud church is situated on a rise above the River Brue and to the south of the town. It is one of two churches founded here before 700; the other – St Peter's – is long gone. Originally this church stood to the north of and within the precincts of Bruton Abbey which has also all but disappeared.

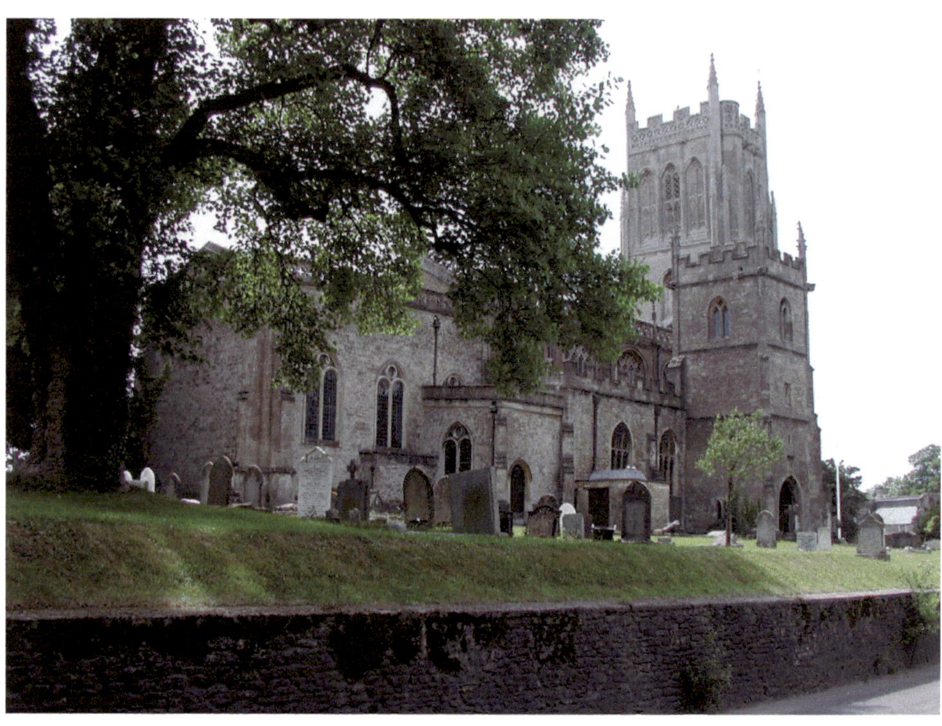

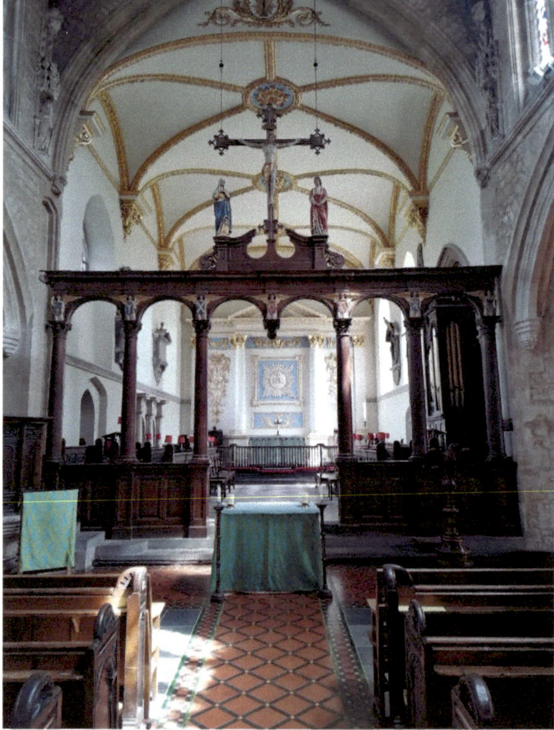

Above: Bruton. The exterior of the eighteenth-century chancel (left) and the two towers.

Left: Bruton. The chancel of 1743 with a screen and rood by W. H. Randoll Blacking, 1938.

Most of the church was rebuilt in the fourteenth and fifteenth centuries, beginning with the north aisle which has a notable tower porch. The next phase was the nave and south aisle together with a new proud west tower. All this is in the Perpendicular style of Gothic. The nave is quite wide and has large clerestory windows separated by image niches. The roof is among Somerset's best, a feat of carpentry with ornate tie beams, panelling and pendant bosses. Lastly, the chancel was rebuilt in 1743, rather plain incorrect Gothic outside with no east window but inside a delightful Rococo composition decorated in blue, white and gold. The groined plaster vault has laurel-leaf ribs and encircled acanthus roses. Tripartite reredos to the east wall with Corinthian columns and central section with pediment and a sunburst. Of interest inside is the monument in the chancel to Sir Maurice Berkeley (d. 1581) and his two wives, recumbent effigies on a tomb chest over which is a heavy canopy with two arched openings. Also in the chancel is a gilded bronze bust to William Godolphin who died at the age of twenty-five in 1636. He was Governor of the Isles of Scilly. The chancel screen and rood are by W. H. Randoll Blacking, 1938. Interestingly the floor of the church slopes up from the tower to the chancel. There is a fourteenth-century vaulted crypt under part of the chancel, three bays long and two bays wide with two pillars to support the groined vault. It also contains lead coffins of the Berkeley family. This is not normally open to the public. The prominent dovecote on the hill to the south, across the railway, is later sixteenth century, after the dissolution of the abbey.

11. BRYMPTON D'EVERCY, ST ANDREW

A long drive leads to Brympton House and the church which lies alongside. Both are built with glorious golden Ham stone. The earliest parts are the late thirteenth-century south doorway and the cusped arch to the south transept. The rest of the cruciform church was built by the end of the fourteenth century. A large and more ornate chapel was added north of the chancel in the later fifteenth century – see the panelled arch between the two. The restoration of 1897 by C. B. Benson saw the panelled ceiling of the south transept moved to the north transept. The chapel's roof, also panelled, is original and has some good bosses but the remaining roofs are of 1897. A notable stone screen is the only division between nave and chancel; the stone seats date from 1897. The spandrels of the screen's central doorway have green men to the nave and dragons on the chancel side. The church has a large collection of monuments, but not all the details can be trusted as J. E. Carew re-carved much of what you see in around 1850. (He is best known for the sculptured panels around Nelson's column in Trafalgar Square, London.) Four of the effigies were originally outside. One of the canopies in the north transept has depictions of the Adoration of the Magi and the Annunciation, both original works. The scenes of the Passion and Crucifixion on the other tomb are by Carew. The standing monument to Sir John Sydenham (d. 1625) is without effigies; its painted tomb chest has a chequer pattern and much heraldry. Openings below reveal a memento mori scene with a collection of sculptured bones in the floor and three skulls under

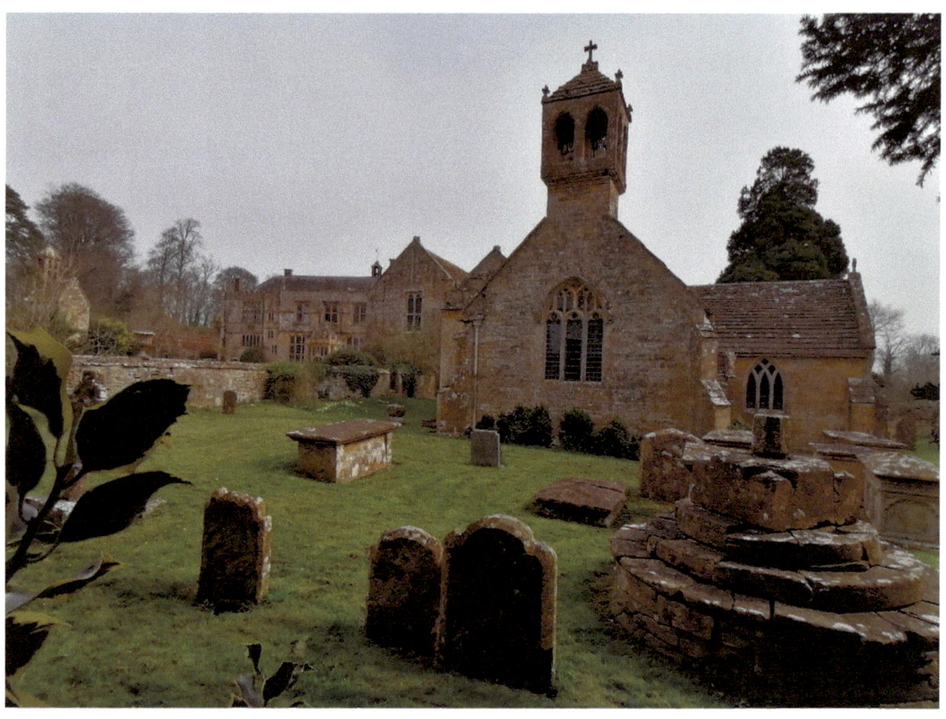

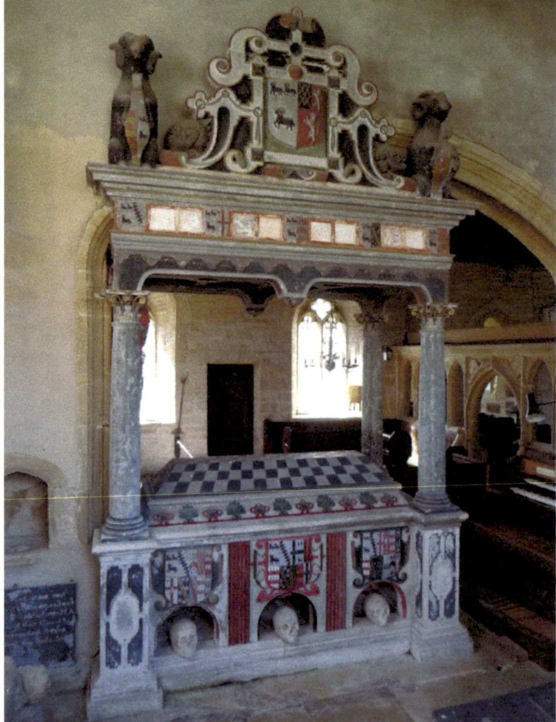

Above: Brympton d'Evercy. Exterior showing the birdcage bellcote and Brympton House next door.

Left: Brympton d'Evercy. The monument to Sir John Sydenham (d. 1625).

these arches on the chapel side. Above, there is a heavy canopy on Corinthian columns with large shields on both sides flanked by Sydenham rams as seen on their coat of arms.

12. CAMELEY, ST JAMES

West of the A37 at Temple Cloud is the small medieval church of Cameley. It consists of a west tower, dating from the fifteenth century, nave with south porch and a chancel. The porch was rebuilt in 1620 and shelters a Norman doorway. Steps up to a door to the west of the porch are a clue to what lies within, an interior which has developed since the Reformation and left unrestored by the Victorians who destroyed many fittings and features in so many other village churches elsewhere. The nave is filled with woodwork: the plain benches (*c.* 1400), the west gallery with balustrade (1711), the south gallery ('Erected for the free Use of the Inhabitants. 1819'), the Jacobean pulpit with tester, reader's desk and family pew (1630) and several box pews which match the south gallery in design. Note also the rows of hat pegs on the nave walls. The chancel has early eighteenth-century Communion rails and reredos. The crude chancel arch, flanked by remains of later altar recesses in the nave, is Norman and is decorated by wall paintings of around 1200, including a royal arms (three lions, north side) and scrolly pattern around the arch. Above, early seventeenth-century Commandment boards surrounded by bands of foliage with amusing cherub heads entwined. The galleries and later wall

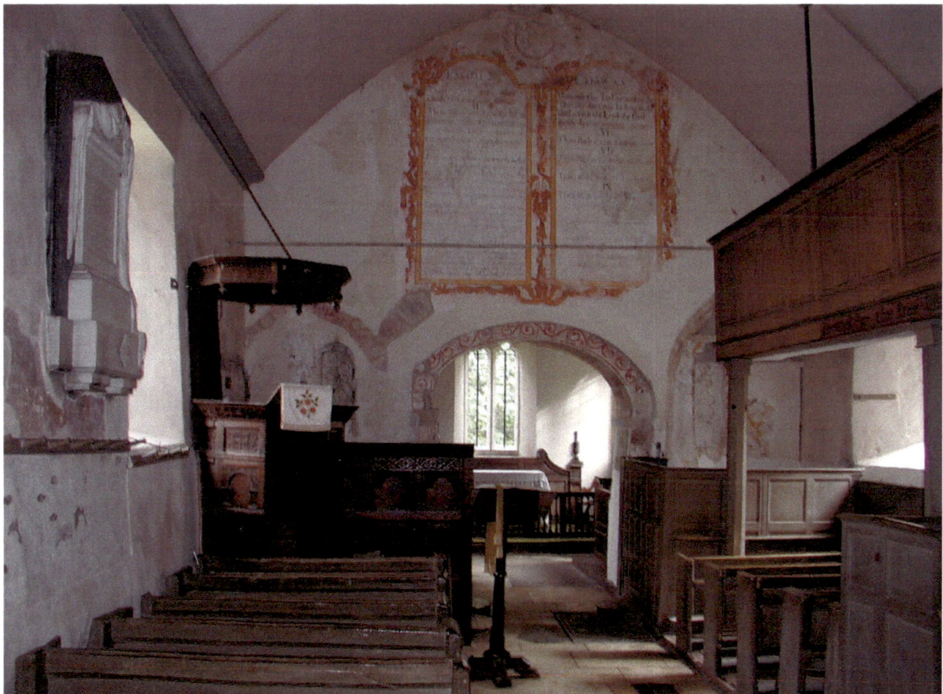

Cameley. The unrestored interior looking east.

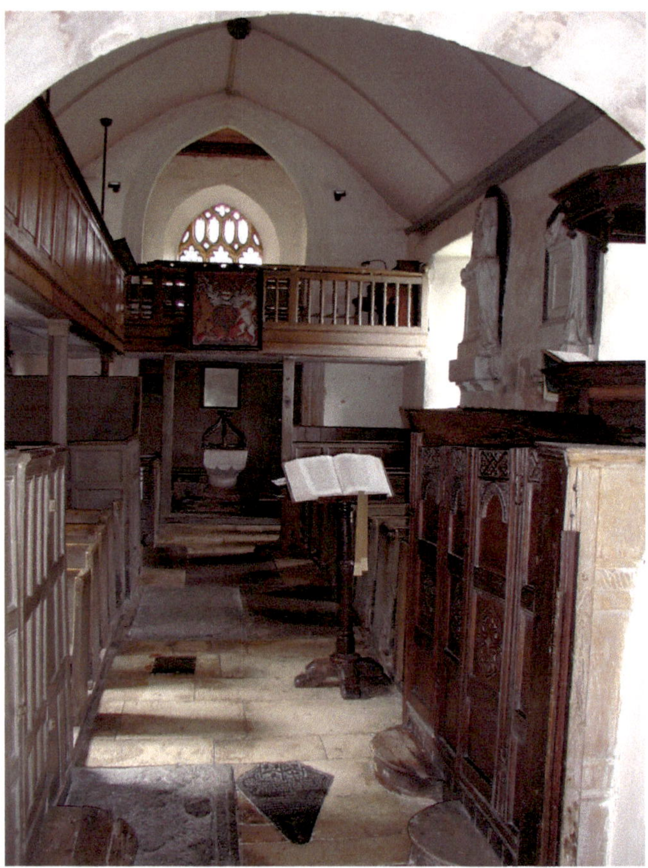

Cameley. Looking west,
charming and cluttered.

monuments have partly destroyed or hidden other wall paintings – a tantalising
foot in a stream with crabs and fish is the remains of a St Christopher (north wall),
and a later royal arms (south wall) are worth mentioning. There is a Norman
font with a Jacobean cover and also an odd wooden head of uncertain date in a
decorative frame which could be as early as tenth-century work but likely later.
The church is no longer in use for regular services but is vested in the Churches
Conservation Trust.

13. Compton Dundon, St Andrew

It is likely that what is now the churchyard has been a site of some form of
worship for over 1,700 years – the age of the giant ancient yew tree which
stands by the path to the south porch. The church mainly dates from the early
fourteenth century, with the porch, nave windows and top stage of the tower
being a century later. The latter has some Norman dogtooth moulding built into
an internal wall, pointing to an earlier building. Three of the four corners of
the church have carved heads outside – who or why is unknown. The panelled
ceilings of the porch and nave are fifteenth century and have carved bosses.

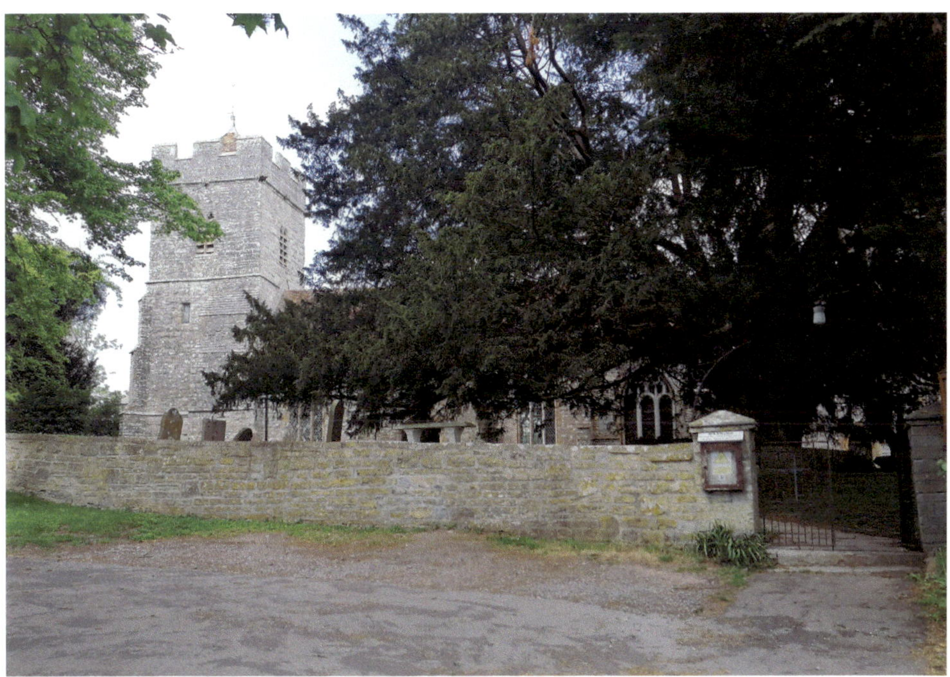

Above: Compton Dundon. The church is dwarfed by its ancient yew tree.

Right: Compton Dundon. The pulpit built into the wall.

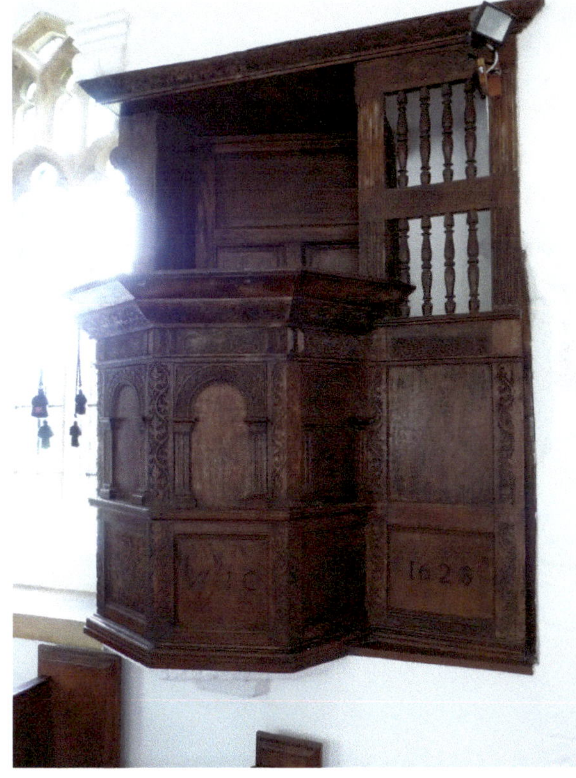

Inside, note the unusual Jacobean pulpit, dated 1628, built into the wall and accessed from the rood stairs, and the low plain stone screen to the chancel. The stained glass in the east window is a memorial to Revd T. W. Harrison (d. 1871); he can be seen bewhiskered in the crowd below. Also of interest are the choir stalls where the front rows can only accommodate children. In the churchyard to the east is a grave marker to a soldier who died a long way from home at Netley military hospital in Hampshire after being injured whilst fighting in the Dardanelles. His family home was in New Zealand, but his parents had lived in Compton Dundon before emigrating. There are wonderful views from the churchyard towards the Polden Hills and of this view Field Marshall Jan Smuts said when he visited on 19 June 1949 that, as an old man, he was glad to have had again this glimpse of Paradise.

14. COMPTON MARTIN, ST MICHAEL AND ALL ANGELS

Placed above the main road through the village with a tall four-staged tower built in the mid-fifteenth century, this is perhaps Somerset's best surviving Norman parish church. Entering the churchyard, the clerestory with its corbel table is clearly visible, *c.* 1150, and points to what will be found inside. The nave has four-bayed arcades with round piers, scalloped capitals and one-stepped arches; note the column on the south side with spiral mouldings similar to those seen

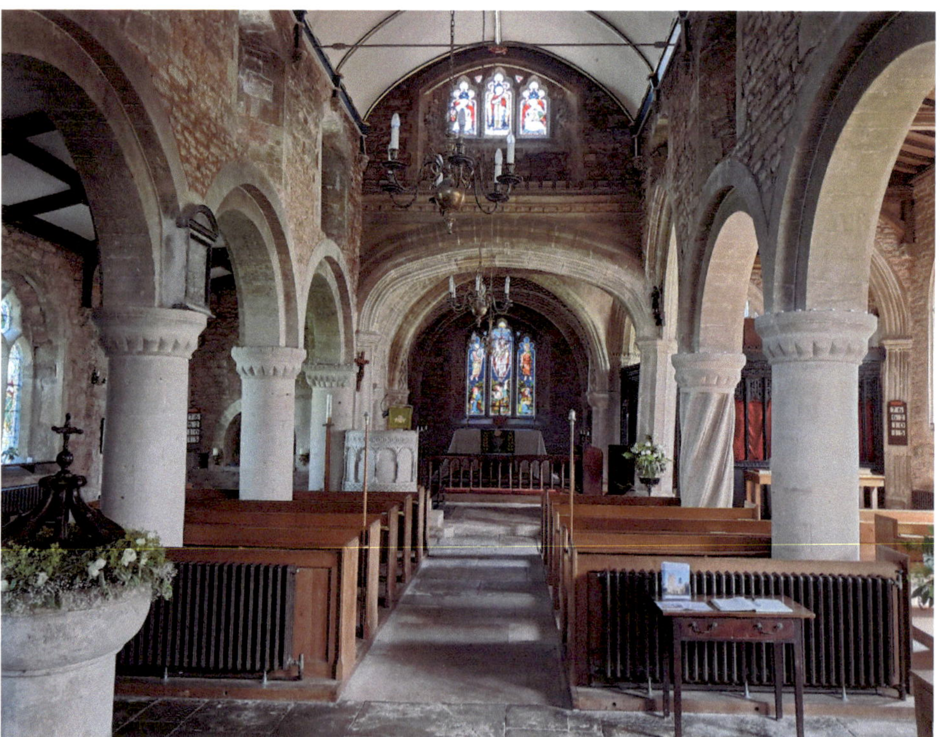

Compton Martin. The interior showing the twisted column.

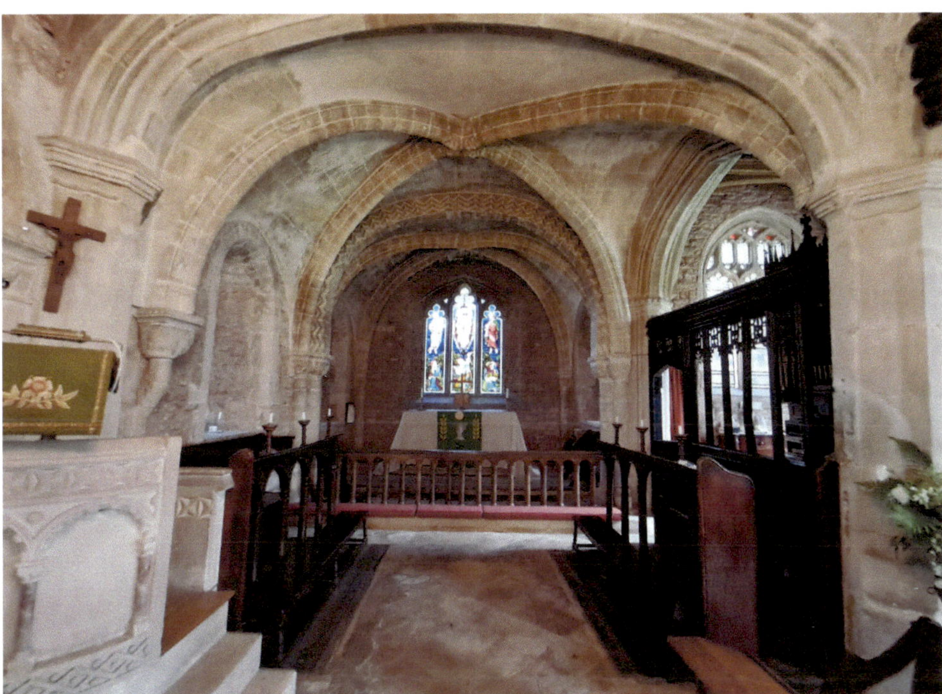

Compton Martin. Close-up of the vaulted chancel.

at Durham Cathedral. The clerestory also survives on the south side but is now inside the church because the south aisle was rebuilt taller and wider after the tower was built. The chancel arch and the adjoining bay of the nave arcade were rebuilt as well but work was abandoned because of subsidence. The chancel is of two bays and is vaulted; note how the ribs of the west bay each terminate in animal heads to form a feature. There is also a Norman pillar piscina but this came from Priddy. It is interesting to see how the altar rails (seventeenth century) echo the Norman theme as do the Victorian choir stalls and pulpit. Don't miss the early effigy (*c.* 1290) at the east end of the north aisle, flatly carved and in a later recess. There is also an unusual feature above the vault in the chancel reached by a door high up in the north wall. It is a pigeon loft, with a separate entrance for the birds, which provided meat for the priest's table.

15. Crewkerne, St Bartholomew

Situated above and to the west of the small town, the church is a cruciform building with a central tower, all rebuilt in the fifteenth and early sixteenth centuries. Approaching from the town, the chancel and transepts are in proportion with the tower, so it is a surprise to see the very lofty clerestoried nave and aisles. Like Yatton (q.v.) the west front has turrets flanking the seven-light west window. The side windows of the aisles are all of six lights, a size not found elsewhere in English parish churches. The south porch is two-storeyed and has a fan vault.

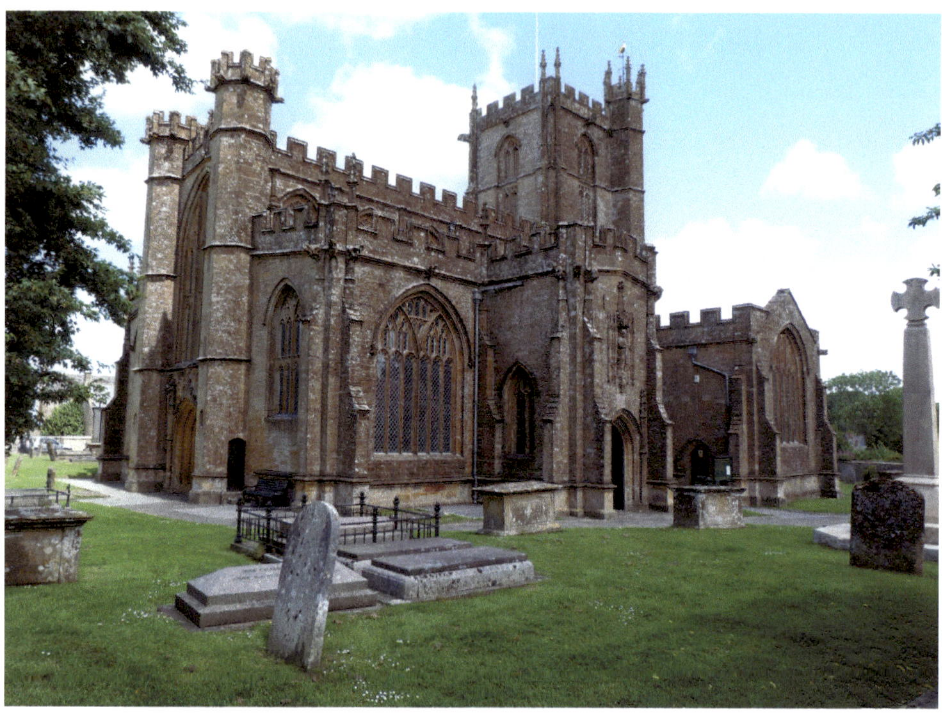

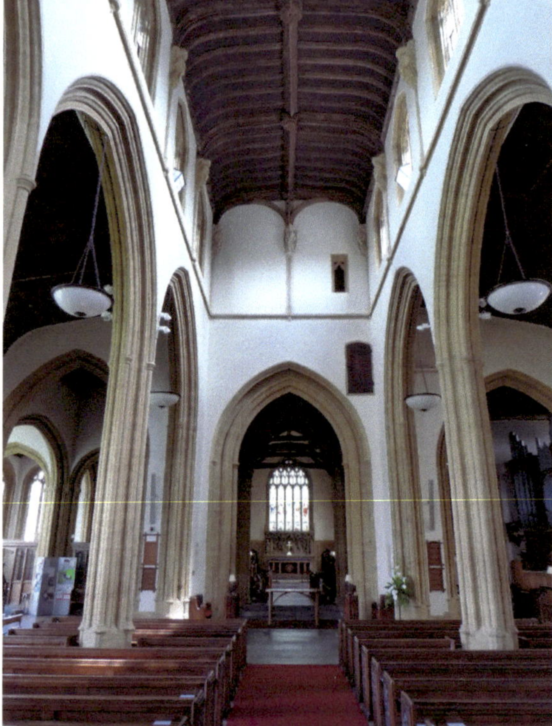

Above: Crewkerne. The aisle windows are among the largest in the country.

Left: Crewkerne. The lofty interior.

Inside the exceptional height of the building is a memorable feature, emphasised by the shortness of the nave. The nave roof has heavy transverse and ridge beams and rests on stone shafts that terminate in standing angels. The remains of the former west gallery at the west end of both aisles date from 1809 to 1811. Above the north gallery is a large royal arms of George III and between them is a fine Tree of Jesse window by A. K. Nicholson (1930). Stone springers under the crossing show the intention to vault the tower; the present fan vault is of wood and was inserted in 1904. The eastern arch contains some fine corbels including a green man on the north side; note the amusing smaller corbels placed above these. In the chancel two medieval doorways flank the reredos of 1902 (with scene of the Last Supper carved by Harry Hems). These doorways have spandrels with hogs on the north and angels on the south; they opened into a sacristy which has since been demolished. Outside in the angle between the south-east buttresses of the transept is what seems to be a doorway (protected by a grille) but was in fact an over-large niche for a statue or sculptured group.

16. CROSCOMBE, ST MARY

The church stands north of the main road and the River Sheppey on a steep hillside. It consists of a nave and chancel with five-bayed aisles together with a two-storeyed treasury south of the tower and a vestry, also originally two-storeyed, at the north-east corner. The south aisle is the earliest part, likely thirteenth-century (see the outer doorway of the south porch) but much altered when the rest was rebuilt *c.* 1420–40; the treasury and vestry were added 1507–09. The tower has diagonal buttresses continued up to four corner pinnacles, battlements with blank arcading, large gargoyles and central image niches, and completed by a recessed spire which had to be rebuilt after it was struck by lightning in 1936. The nave and chancel have battlements and pinnacles, while the rest has parapets with close blank arcading. Inside, the church has arcades of five bays which reuse fourteenth-century columns and the low tower arch is also fourteenth century. An awkward fan vault has been inserted under the tower, probably *c.* 1500 or later. Unusually the chancel arch springs from corbels in the spandrels of the arcade and the roofs differ each side, in the nave is a wagon roof panelled with large lozenge-shaped bosses and winged angels against the wall plates, the chancel has a tie beam roof which was remodelled in 1664 when all the knobbly decoration was applied. The glory of Croscombe is its woodwork, perhaps the best surviving Jacobean interior in England. The chancel screen is exceptionally tall and has two tiers of two-light openings divided by slender Ionic columns (the arches in the openings join in a pendant rather than a column). Above there is a panelled entablature surmounted by many obelisks and open strapwork and, in the centre, the royal arms of James I with its own entablature, strapwork and obelisks where a medieval screen would have had the rood figures. Below the central archway has naked figures in the spandrels. There are matching readers desks (with amusing caryatids), stalls and parclose screens, the latter richly carved. In the nave is a mixture of Jacobean box pews, box pews with reused medieval ends, and seating of 1836 in the aisles. All of the Jacobean woodwork was given *c.* 1616 by Hugh Fortescue, Lord of the Manor,

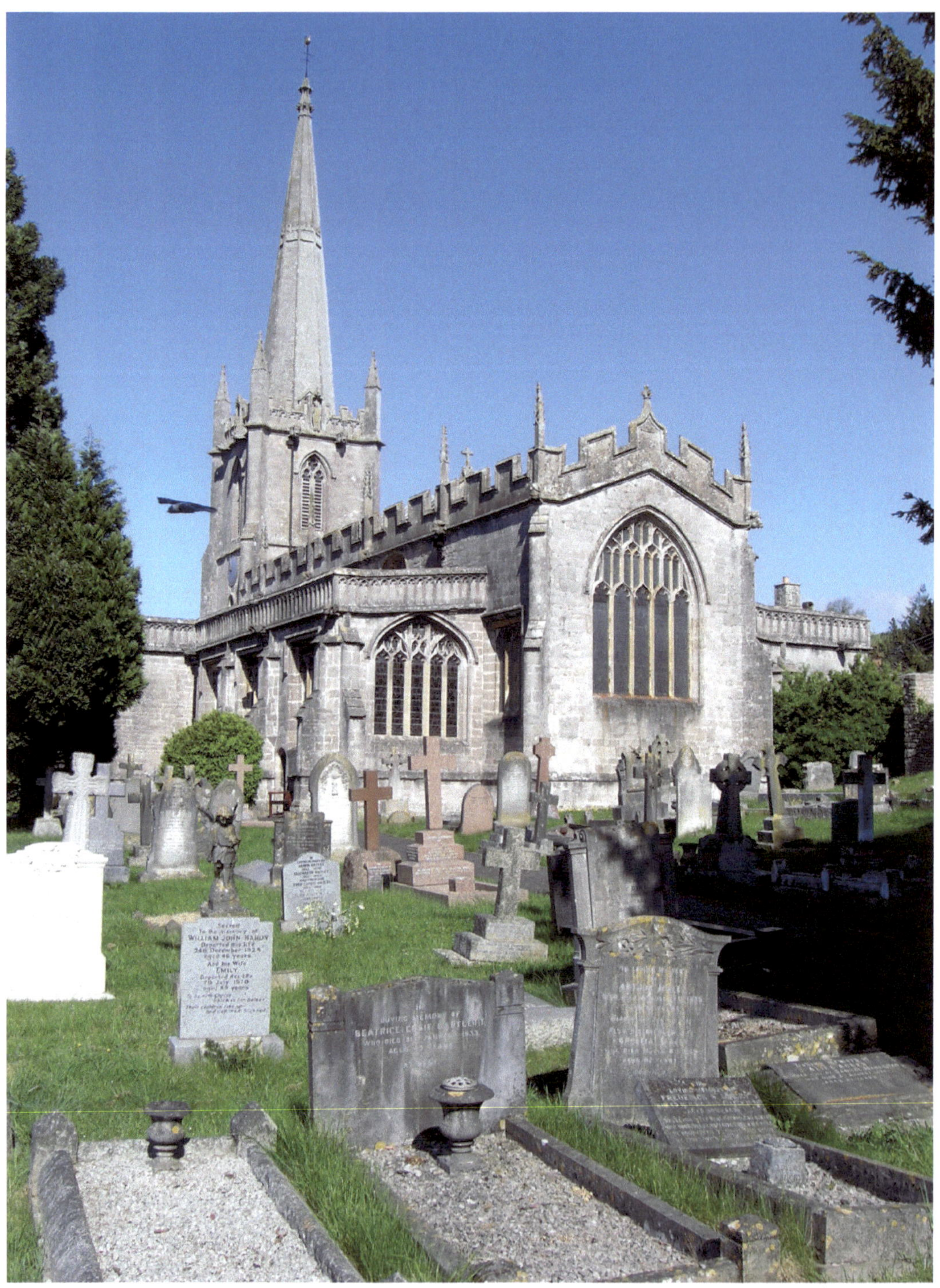

Croscombe. From the south-east. The spire was struck by lightning in 1936.

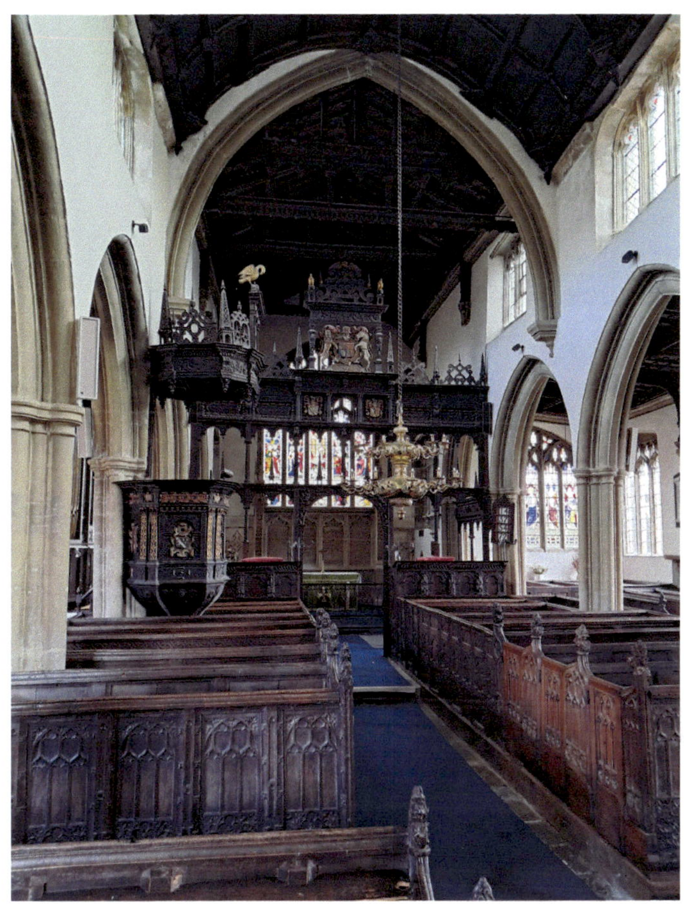

Croscombe. Dark woodwork dominates the interior.

with the exception of the matching pulpit and tester, actually dated 1616, the gift of Bishop Lake of Bath & Wells whose arms are carried atop the tester along with a gilded pelican. There are two brasses in the south aisle to kneeling members of the Bisse family, to James (d. 1606), his wife and twelve children, and to William (d. 1625) and his eighteen children; both families had equal numbers of sons and daughters! The treasury has closely barred small windows to the lower floor and a staircase to the upper floor which was the meeting room for the various guilds associated with the church. The vestry, reached by a small passageway from the north aisle, has lost its upper floor so the room is now open to the thick-ribbed tunnel vault. Both these areas are usually kept locked.

17. CULBONE, ST BEUNO

St Beuno is the smallest complete medieval church in England – that is to say, nave, chancel and south porch – and stands in almost complete isolation in a wooded valley. There is no road access and most people walk the two miles from Porlock Weir along the South West Coast Path. It is also possible to walk downhill

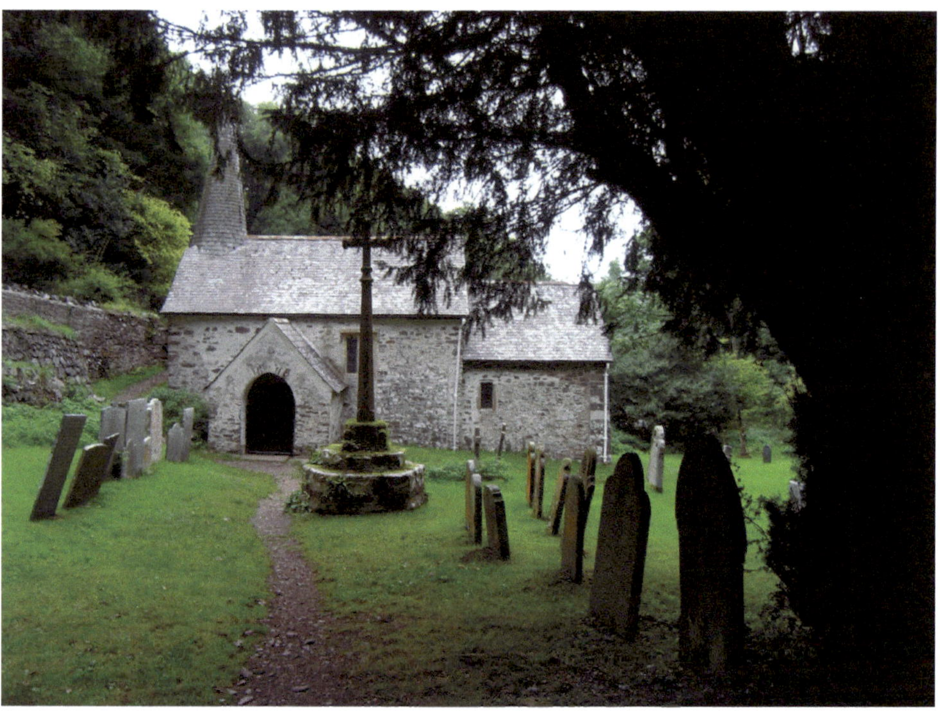

Above: Culbone. The sylvan setting of England's smallest church.

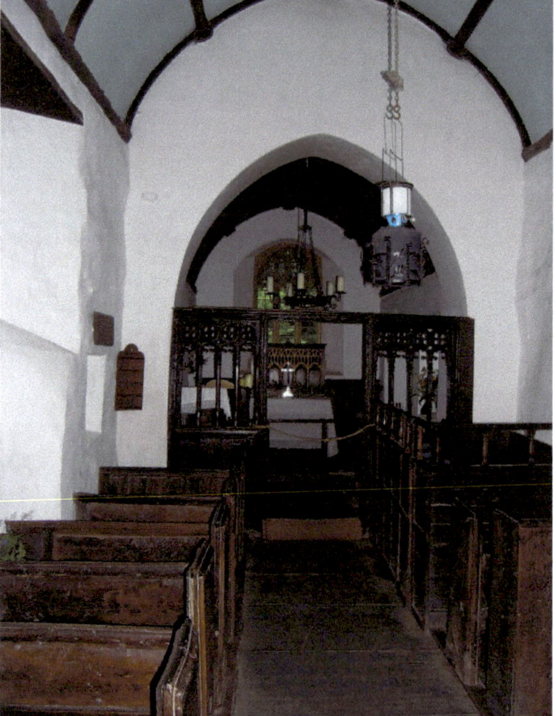

Left: Culbone. The humble interior. The benches just about accommodate a couple.

from Silcombe Farm to the west but there is little car parking here. Both routes can be quite arduous and be sure to take refreshments. It is not the architecture that draws visitors here but the setting, picturesque and peaceful. The church is of some antiquity, see the herringbone masonry in the chancel, typical of the late Saxon to early Norman period. On the north side is a Norman window, its two lights divided by a crude pilaster which is topped by a grotesque mask. The fifteenth-century nave north window is made of wood. Inside are tiny old benches and a simple screen, also fifteenth century, the doorway flanked by four-light traceried openings. A little later is the family pew with balustraded top. The tiny slate spire was added in the early nineteenth century and straddles the apex of the roof. Its appearance, and that of nearby Porlock church missing the top of its spire, has sparked many legends!

In the same benefice is Oare where the simple much-restored church and valley are steeped in the story of Lorna Doone.

18. DOWNSIDE ABBEY, ST GREGORY THE GREAT

This Roman Catholic cathedral-sized church is in the village of Stratton-on-the-Fosse. The Benedictine community was founded in 1605 in Douai in Flanders where priests were trained for service in England, Wales, Scotland and Ireland after the Reformation. The monks were expelled from Douai in 1793 and found a home first at Acton Burnell Hall in Shropshire before moving to Downside House in 1814 where they established a school. The first church, built in 1823 alongside the house, still survives as part of the Old School and, like the abbey's domestic buildings and cloisters, is closed to visitors.

Work began on a vast new church to the designs of the firm Dunn & Hansom in 1873 with construction of the transepts (including the lower stages of the south tower), crossing and adjacent bays and chapels. The church thus far was opened in 1882. In 1886 attention shifted to the east end chapels and the apsidal Lady Chapel was consecrated in 1888. The rest of the chapels were completed by F. A. Walters, but the two on the south side were given straight east ends. The south choir aisle was also built to connect the east end to the south transept. The next phase was the completion of the choir 1901–05, a further six bays, the windows with Perpendicular tracery, and terminating in a straight east end. The architect was Thomas Garner, who died the year following completion and is buried here; his monument designed by F. A. Walters is in the north choir aisle. Work resumed again 1923–25 when the nave was added by Giles Gilbert Scott but it was never completed – see the temporary west wall and the sudden termination of the arcades which were to have been ten bays long. Scott then completed Dunn & Hansom's tower (1937–38) by adding a third stage, parapet and pinnacles to make it Somerset's second tallest tower after Wells Cathedral's central tower. Originally it was to have an even taller spire. The whole church is vaulted and, despite being the work of four different architectural practices, it seems remarkably uniform at a quick glance, but closer inspection reveals the differences in design and style. This echoes the building of many of our great churches and cathedrals from medieval times. The Lady Chapel fittings and stained glass are all

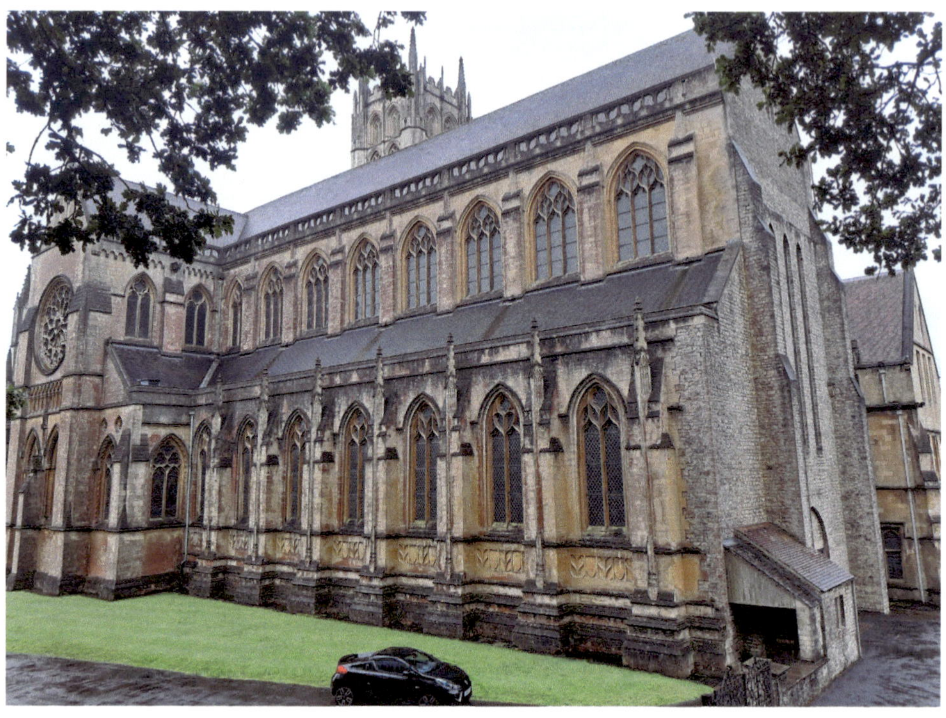

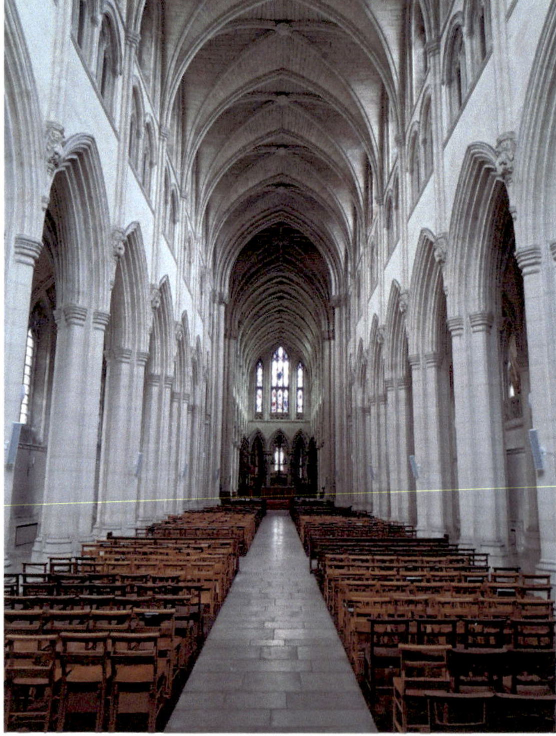

Above: Downside Abbey. The grand exterior showing the incomplete west end.

Left: Downside Abbey. The soaring vaulted interior looking east.

the work of Sir Ninian Comper and he, Walters and Scott provided most of the other fittings, most notably Scott's choir stalls of 1931–33 which recall those in Chester Cathedral. However, there are also some medieval fittings donated to the abbey largely in the north choir chapels, including a Flemish triptych of *c.* 1540 and a German panel of the Crucifixion set in the centre of a reredos by Hansom. All at the abbey impresses greatly with the exception of the main public entrance which is a shed-like lean-to structure at the west end of the north aisle.

The last monks moved out in 2022, ending a way of life here which had lasted for over 200 years, but the school continues to flourish. On the main road is another small Catholic church (St Benedict) built in 1857 for the village. It is still used today.

19. DUNSTER, ST GEORGE

The church stands close to the castle at the top of the long main street which is thronged by visitors in the summer months. The church was given to the monks of Bath before 1100 and they established a priory and set about rebuilding the church of which little remains apart from the partly reconstructed west doorway and the piers supporting the central tower. The chancel is thirteenth century, although much of the detail is the work of George Edmund Street who replaced the east window with three stepped lancets during his restoration of the church

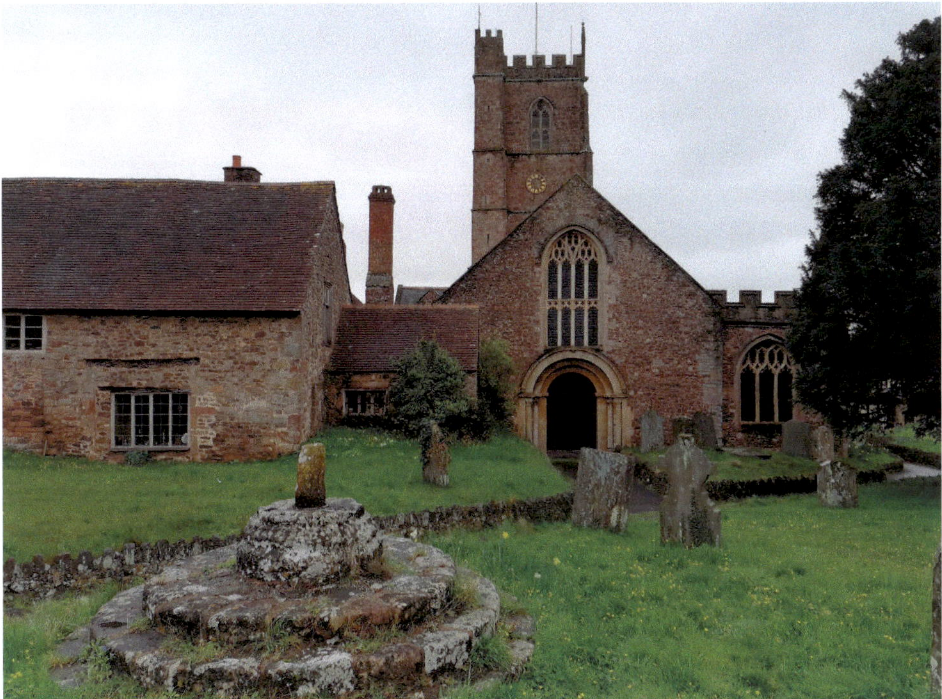

Dunster. The priory buildings from the west with the base of a fifteenth-century churchyard cross.

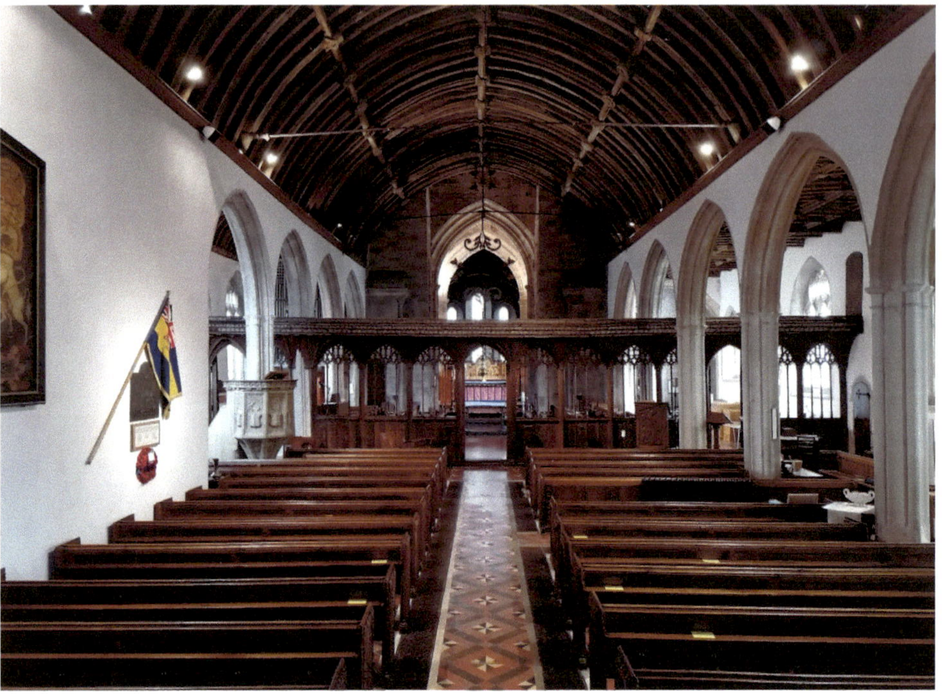

Dunster. The interior looking east and showing the screen across nave and aisles.

in 1875–77. The rest of the church dates from *c*. 1450–1500, seemingly begun by raising the tall central tower. The south aisle has a six-bayed arcade while the north has four because the priory buildings adjoined the west end of the church. The nave was parochial; the choir belonged to the monks. This shared arrangement was not always a happy one and a dispute arose about who used which part that was settled in 1498. This led to the parish constructing the rood screen two bays west of the crossing and placing their high altar under the west crossing arch. The church was not united as one after the dissolution of the priory in 1539 as the east end passed into the ownership of the Luttrell family at the castle. Street screened off the monastic choir and arranged it like a college chapel with side facing seating. The parochial high altar was moved close to the east crossing arch and Street created a chancel in the two east bays of the nave with parclose screens, stalls and encaustic tiled floor. There are several monuments in the church but the most interesting is a swagger monument in the south chapel to Thomas Luttrell (d. 1571), his wife and George Luttrell (d. 1629) and wife. George is shown kneeling; the others are recumbent as George erected this monument in 1613 following the death of his wife. His inscription panel below is left blank. Don't miss the bizarre arch into the south chapel from the transept. The screen in the nave dates from around 1500 and spans nave and both aisles. It was originally painted. Similar screens can be found nearby at St Michael's Church in Minehead and Carhampton Church, probably made by the same craftsmen. The latter is still painted.

20. EAST BRENT, ST MARY THE VIRGIN

The church stands at the foot of Brent Knoll and has a disproportionately tall five-staged tower with recessed spire, all quite plain, apart from the pierced parapet. The west side has three tiers of niches with original statues, the Virgin and Child, God the Father holding the Crucified Christ and Christ crowning the Virgin, a rare survival. The base of the tower with its crude arch and the nave are probably the oldest parts, but no features survive to help dating. Subsequent additions and rebuilding have altered the church. The porch is late thirteenth century, the two-bayed south chapel to the east is later fourteenth century and the fine north aisle with its openwork parapet and arcade are later fifteenth century. The chancel was largely rebuilt in the nineteenth century. The most memorable feature inside is the nave's plaster ceiling, dated 1637 on one of the pendant bosses, and is almost certainly by George Drayton (*see* Axbridge). It rests on medieval corbels and the rood-loft window on the south side is also older. The pulpit and west gallery are from the same period but other woodwork is earlier, including a fine set of bench ends and one of only twenty-one surviving wooden lecterns in the country with a big eagle on a large baluster and now seemingly out of favour in the north aisle – a new, plain, modern lectern now stands by the chancel arch. In the north aisle is a

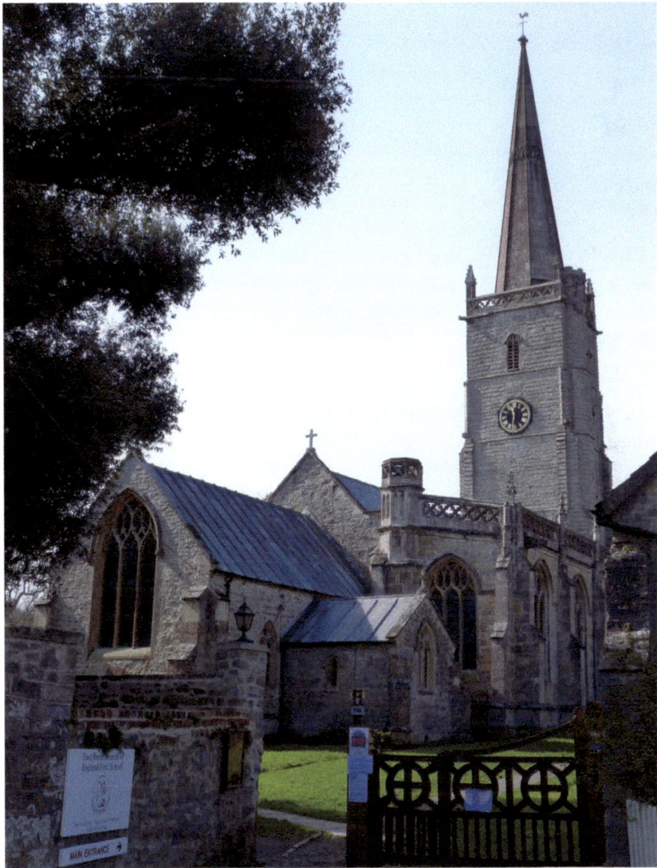

East Brent. The church is dominated by its tall slim tower and spire.

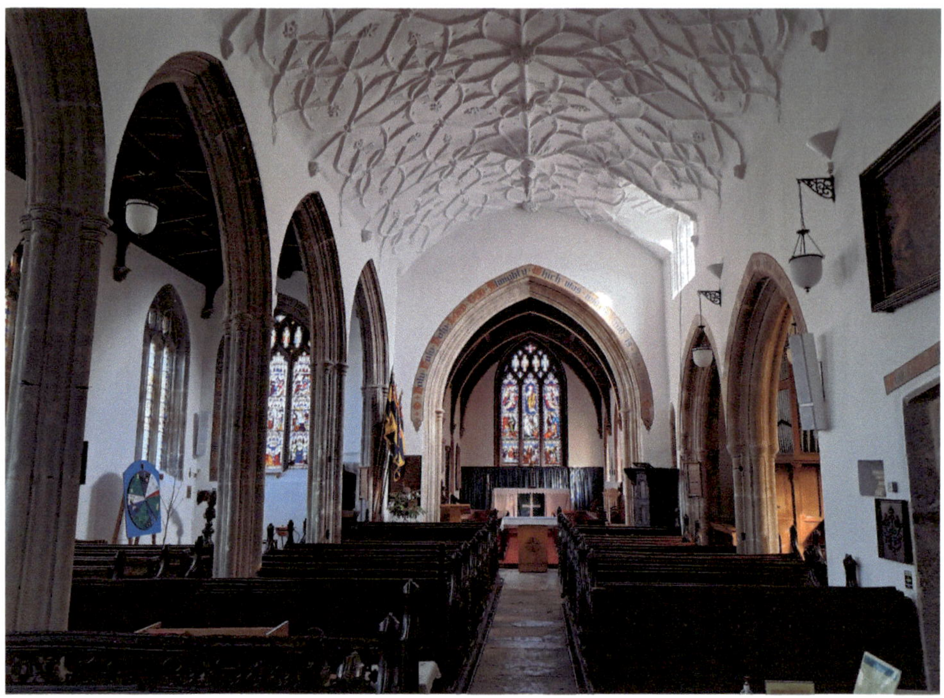

East Brent. The plaster ceiling dates from 1637 and is similar to nearby Axbridge.

worn effigy of a priest and there is another in the south chapel, better preserved. Here too, a large Victorian Gothic hanging monument to three children who pre-deceased their parents who are also commemorated below. The east window of the north aisle has stained glass with nine colourful scenes. It appears to be early fifteenth century, but some experts have cast doubt on this. However, the three saints in the window to the left are medieval and were the inspiration for the rest of the north windows by Joseph Bell of Bristol from the mid-nineteenth century.

On the other side of the hill is Brent Knoll, originally South Brent, where the church has some remarkable bench ends probably by the same sculptor as East Brent.

21. GLASTONBURY, ST JOHN THE BAPTIST

The tall tower of this church dwarfs that of the town's second medieval church of St Benedict and is the second tallest in Somerset at 134 feet (41m). It was the last part of the church to be built (*c.* 1500) and is finished by an openwork crown of battlements and pinnacles, as at Dundry and Taunton and first seen at Gloucester Cathedral. Viewed face on, the tower presents an unusual outline as the pinnacles flanking the top stage sit on top of the setback buttresses but are only joined to the tower walls by tiny flying buttresses. The church lies along the north side of the High Street and the churchyard is usually a meeting place for many of the colourful characters who call this place home. In medieval times this church in turn was dwarfed by the huge abbey church with its three towers and, of course, the

Tor crowned by the chapel of St Michael, of which the ornate tower survives. The lofty and spacious nave and aisles have seven-bayed arcades and a fine roof (much restored) with tie beams. The vaulted south porch is earlier fifteenth-century but the upper room with its four-light window is of *c.* 1500. The chancel is lower and has two-bayed arcades and a large seven-light east window. There is medieval glass in both side windows in the sanctuary, reassembled from fragments. The church has been reordered inside and several items have been moved to new locations.

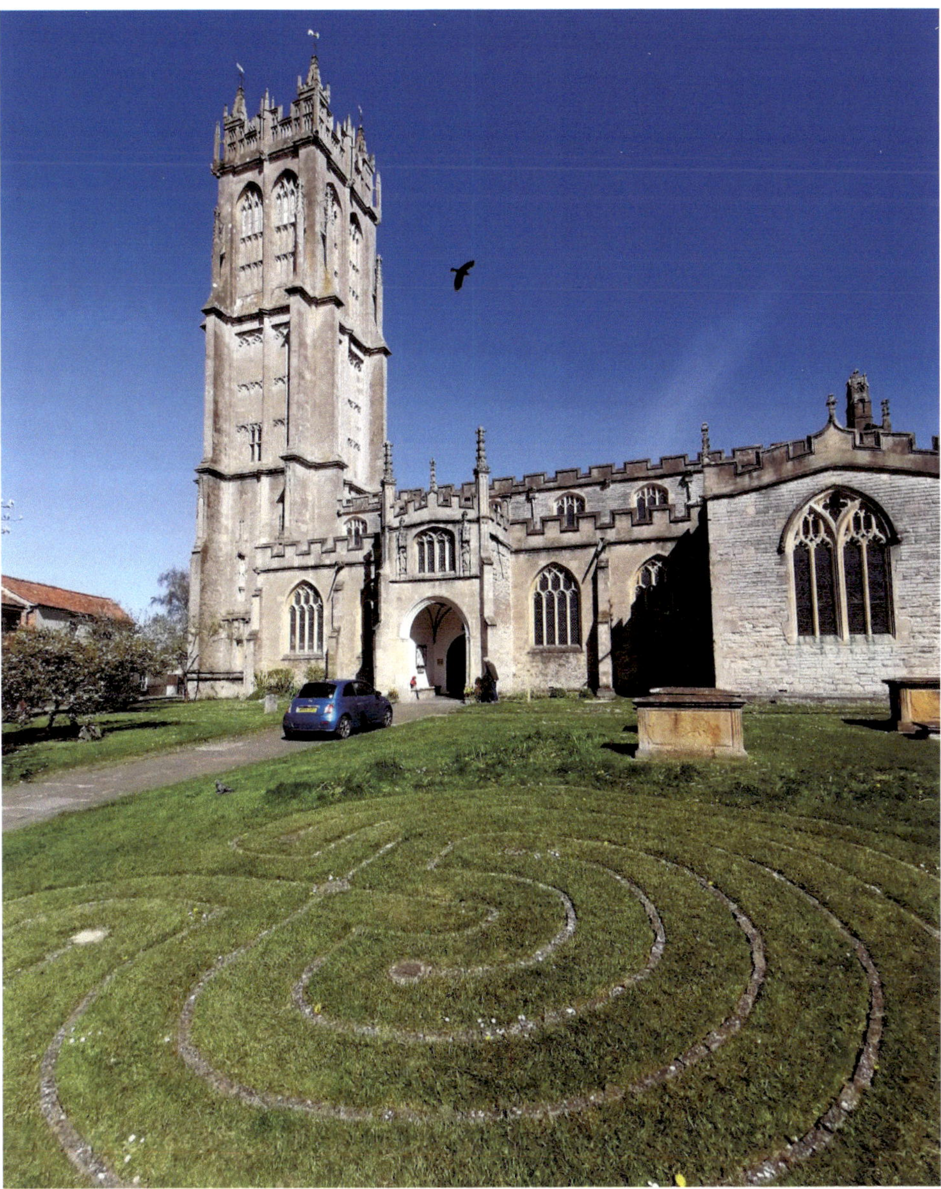

Glastonbury. St John the Baptist. The churchyard grass often has a maze cut into it.

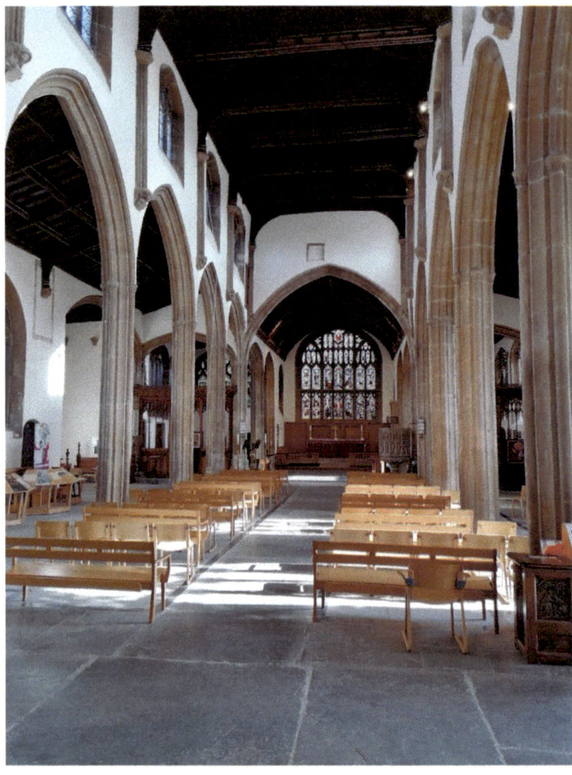

Glastonbury. St John the Baptist.
The interior was recently restored
and underfloor heating installed.

Gone are the heavy constricting wooden pews in the nave and aisles which
enabled the very fine tomb chest decorated with panels containing shield-holding
angels and camels to be moved from under the north arcade to a freestanding
position in the north aisle. On top is the alabaster effigy of John Camel (d. 1487)
in civilian dress with much medieval colour. There is a purse hanging from his belt
and his head is supported by angels. Two more tomb chests stand in the chancel,
their Purbeck marble tops having matrices of lost brasses. The font has moved into
the north chapel and the fine stone pulpit has swapped sides at the chancel arch;
both are by George Gilbert Scott who restored the church in 1856–57. The fine
screens remain in situ; most date from the first quarter of the twentieth century
but incorporated into the south transept screen of 1929 are medieval headpieces
retrieved from both the museum and built into houses in Northload Street. The
blind upper tracery of these two-light divisions are carved with a rose, a paschal
lamb, a pelican and what is probably St George.

22. GOATHURST, ST EDWARD

The path from the lychgate to the church porch passes by a most remarkable
monument to John Willis (d. 1725), an ornate table tomb surmounted by
a tapering Corinthian column, and all restored 2024–25 by Sally Strachan
Conservation. The bulky plain tower is built from siltstones and dates from the

fifteenth century like most of the rest of the church. The exception is the north chapel, which was built after 1559 by Sir Nicholas Halswell to house their family monuments, but these are hidden from the initial view of the interior. Under the tower eight painted panels are preserved from a former gallery. The south transept was remodelled in 1758 to serve as the Halswell family pew and has a pretty plaster ceiling. In the nave are two large hanging monuments, one by Rysbrack with a bust, the other by Nollekens with a mourning female and portrait medallion. The pulpit is early seventeenth century with a large tester above of *c.* 1700. Two large standing monuments dominate the north chapel; in the north-west corner the finely detailed effigies of Sir Nicholas Halswell (d. 1633) and wife lie under an

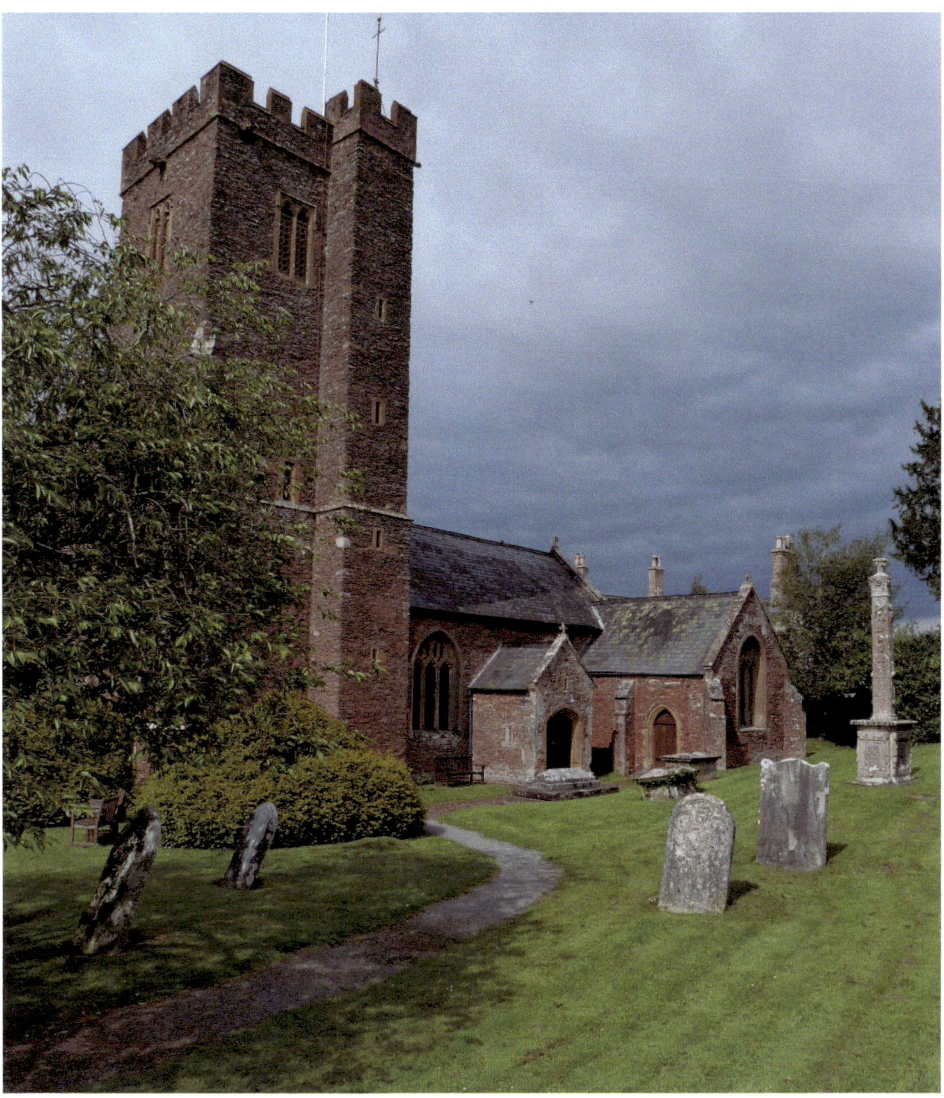

Goathurst. The remarkable monument to John Willis (d. 1725) is shown on the right.

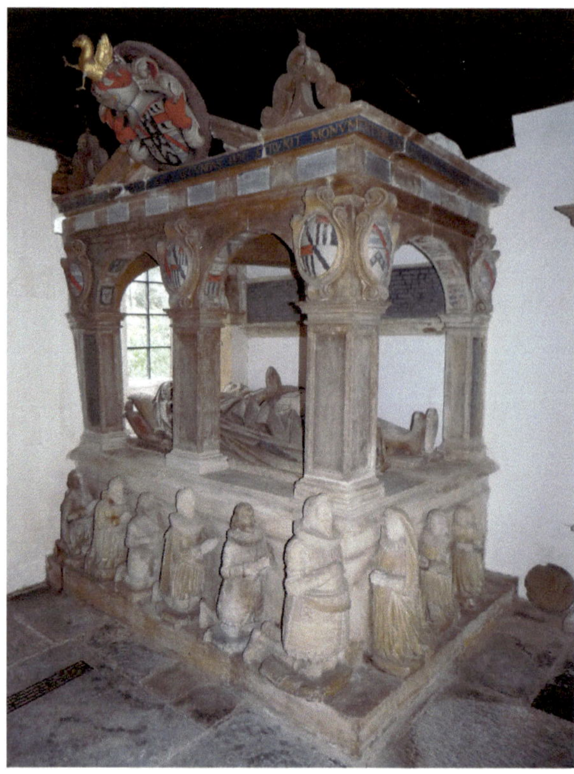

Goathurst. A small window
lights the effigies of Sir Nicholas
Halswell (d. 1633) and his wife.

arched canopy, the tomb chest embellished by kneeling figures of their children,
six sons on the long side and three daughters on the short side. Small panels on the
canopy above name the children below, and the crowning crest leaning forward
seems to defy gravity! Sir Nicholas was a local magistrate and presided over the
bizarre case of John Gilbert, a minister arrested for attempting to preach naked
on the Sabbath at North Petherton Church in 1608! The other monument is to
the Halswell family with a lengthy inscription in Latin flanked by two standing
allegorical figures and with two cheerful putti on the broken pediment above.
Finally, poorly sited on on the floor in the north-east corner, is a moving white
marble depiction of a sleeping child, three-year-old Isabella Cooper (1838) by the
Irish sculptor Christopher Moore.

23. HINTON ST GEORGE, ST GEORGE

The church is built of golden Ham stone, like the rest of this attractive village.
It dates from the later fifteenth century and consists of a west tower, nave with south
aisle and porch and chancel with side chapels and a vestry at the north-east. There
is also a north transept, rebuilt in 1814 by Jeffry Wyatt as a family pew for the
Poulet family and raised over a burial vault. To the east of the transept the Poulet
chapel was rebuilt at the same time. (Wyatt was later knighted and changed his
surname to Wyatville; he most famously worked at restoring and rebuilding much

of Windsor Castle and Chatsworth House.) The west tower is similar to Norton-sub-Hamdon and Crewkerne, with the bell openings extending through the top two stages. Above is an ornate openwork parapet bristling with pinnacles and the south-east stair turret has its own similar parapet and pinnacles. The south porch has a pointed panelled tunnel vault. Inside the nave and aisle roofs are original late-fifteenth-century work but the chancel has a plaster vault painted to resemble stone, likely dating from 1814. The nave and north transept have many monuments with busts or portrait medallions from the eighteenth and nineteenth centuries. By the steps up to the family pew is a tomb chest with a good effigy of a knight, his feet on a lively dog, and with much medieval colour, and by it, to the east, a late fifteenth-century brass with figures of John Chudderle and his wife. Entering the chancel, on the left is a large tomb chest with the effigies of Sir Anthony Poulet (d. 1600) and his wife lying under a large canopy looking up at a coffered ceiling. Their children kneel against the chest and are named in little inscriptions. It opens into the Poulett Chapel and tantalising glimpses of the monuments therein can be made through the arch from the chancel. The chapel is entered from the family pew which retains much of its upholstered furniture. On the north wall twin monuments each with a pair of effigies in ornate recesses; note the small now headless figures kneeling behind little lecterns along the tops of the chests. Against the west wall the monument to Sir Amyas Poulet (d. 1588), an alabaster effigy lying on a rolled-up mat, is unusual as it was brought here from St Martin-in-the-Fields, London, in 1728. The top section is a later memorial but seems to be an integral part.

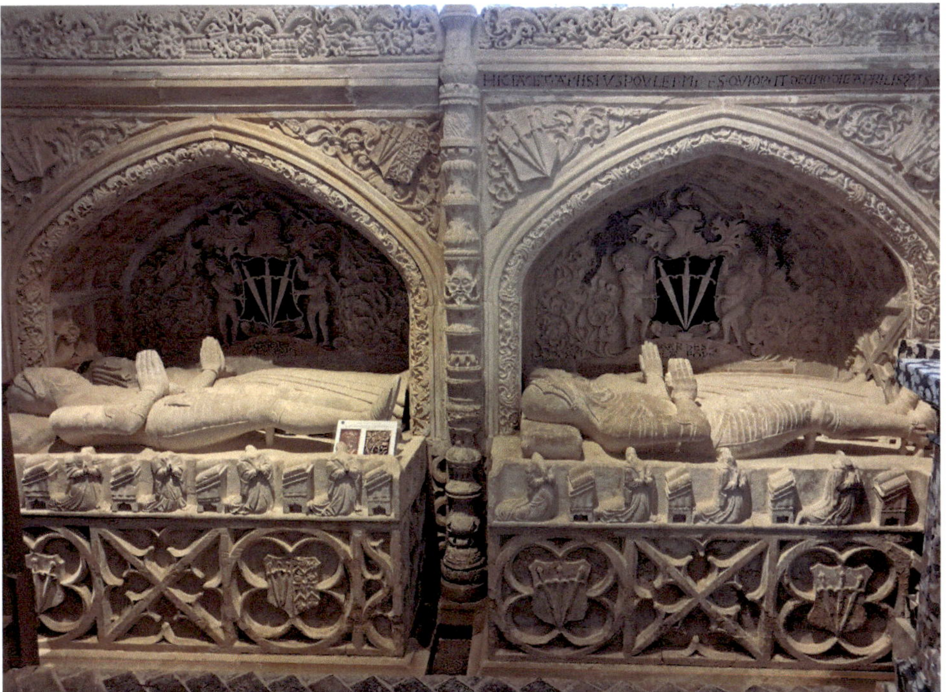

Hinton St George. Near twin monuments in the Poulett Chapel.

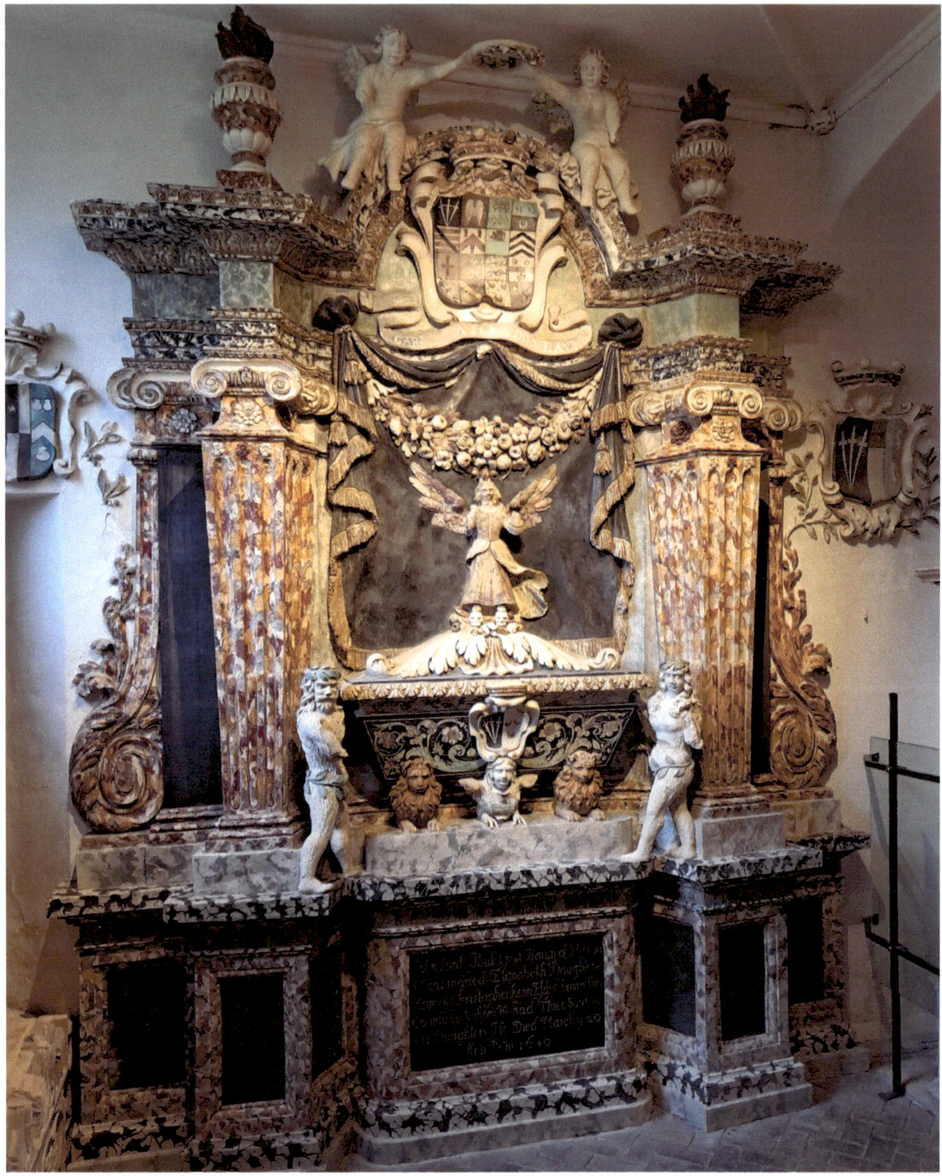

Hinton St George. Poulett Chapel. Monument showing the first use of scagliola in England.

Finally, against the east wall is John, Baron Poulett (d. 1649), a remarkable piece of art, made from plaster. Pigments were used to give the effect of marble, known as scagliola. It is very fragile and is a major reason why this chapel is kept locked today. When I first saw this monument in 2007 both the wild man and wild woman (part of the Poulett crest) had both arms. The central figure, standing on skulls, is Fame and once had trumpets. It is recommended that you arrange access to the chapel before you visit to avoid disappointment (01460 76406).

24. ILMINSTER, ST MARY THE VIRGIN

Now referred to as 'the Minster', the parish church was entirely rebuilt in the latter half of the fifteenth century. The central tower recalls the central tower at Wells Cathedral. It has twelve pinnacles, including a larger taller turret at the north-west angle above the stairs. The church is raised above the street and there is a fine south porch but today the main entrance is via the west door. However, it is worth walking around to the north side of the church to admire the exterior of the ornate north transept, which at the latest is fifteenth century. In 1824–25, in order to increase capacity, William Burgess of Exeter altered the nave and aisles so that galleries could be built. The pillars were raised along with the aisles and the arcade reduced from five to three bays as were the corresponding clerestory windows above. The former roofline can be seen above the west crossing arch. The galleries were removed in 1902 and a smaller west gallery built under which is the main entrance vestibule. The doors into the nave, engraved by Tracey Sheppard, were provided to mark the Millenium. Burgess's flat ceiling to the nave was replaced in 1934. The stately pulpit dates from the seventeenth century and has panels flanked by fluted Ionic columns. The four arches supporting the tower are panelled and the crossing has a fan vault. In the north transept is a very large mutilated tomb chest with the brasses of Sir William Wadham (d. 1452) and his mother. Both appear again on the end of the tomb chest kneeling either side of a seated figure of Christ surrounded by a sunburst. There is also another large tomb chest in the corner of the transept with an architectural back wall and very fine

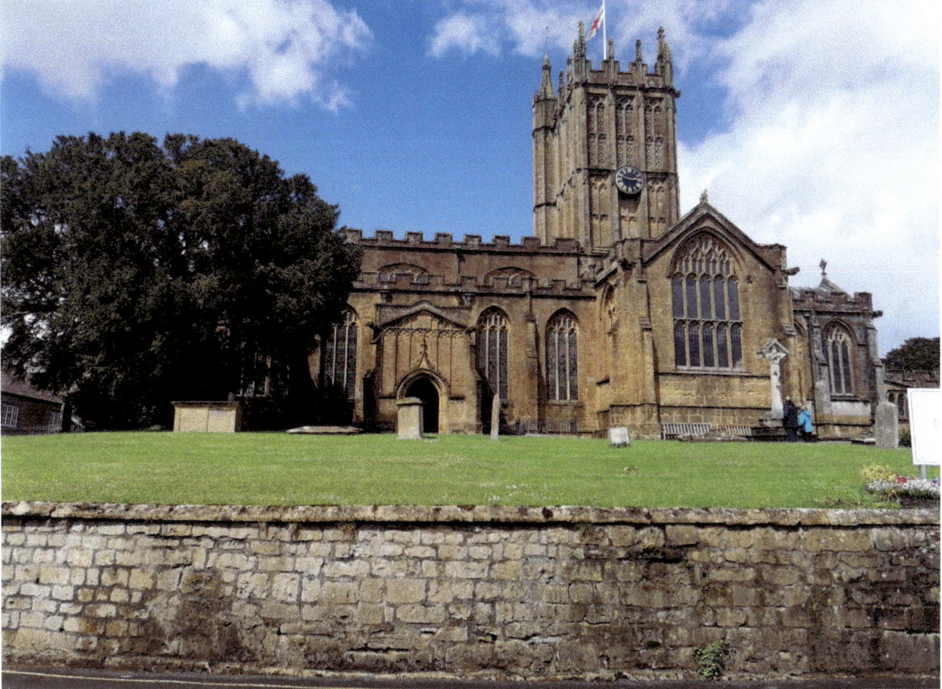

Ilminster. The church is raised above Silver Street.

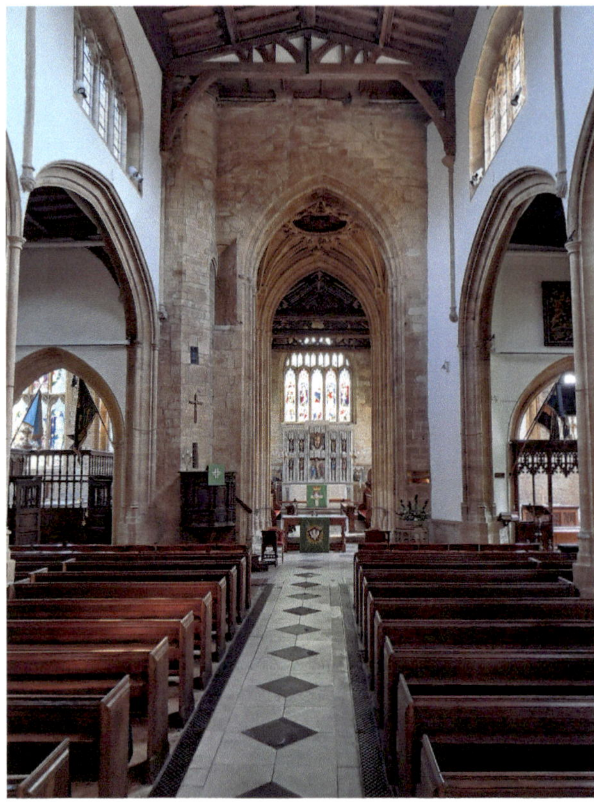

Ilminster. The interior was
altered in Georgian times.

brass figures, to Nicholas Wadham (d. 1609) and Dorothy Wadham (d. 1618), the
founders of Wadham College in Oxford. He is in armour and his wife is in gown
and head-dress. The screen to the transept was adapted from seventeenth-century
work in around 1700 – see the Jacobean panel above the doorway. The chancel
seems rather bare but has a notable stone reredos of 1913 by Frederick Bligh
Bond, the figures painted in 1954. The flanking doors lead into a low east vestry
below the window and are medieval.

25. Isle Abbots, St Mary the Virgin

This church stands in an isolated spot close to the River Isle, the village itself being
reached by a no-through road. The church tower presents itself to the road, the
church is attached behind. This is perhaps the best tower in Somerset and has a
near twin at Kingston St Mary, north of Taunton. This west face is faced with
honey-coloured Ham stone, the other three sides are mainly of local blue lias with
Ham stone dressings. Perhaps because of the remoteness of the village, the tower
still has most of its original statues, a precious survival, including the Virgin with
Child and Jesus rising from the tomb flanking the west window. At the base of
the ornate pierced parapet are eight hunky punks, a local term meaning mainly
small animals but at the north-west angle a piper plays a double-barrelled bagpipe.

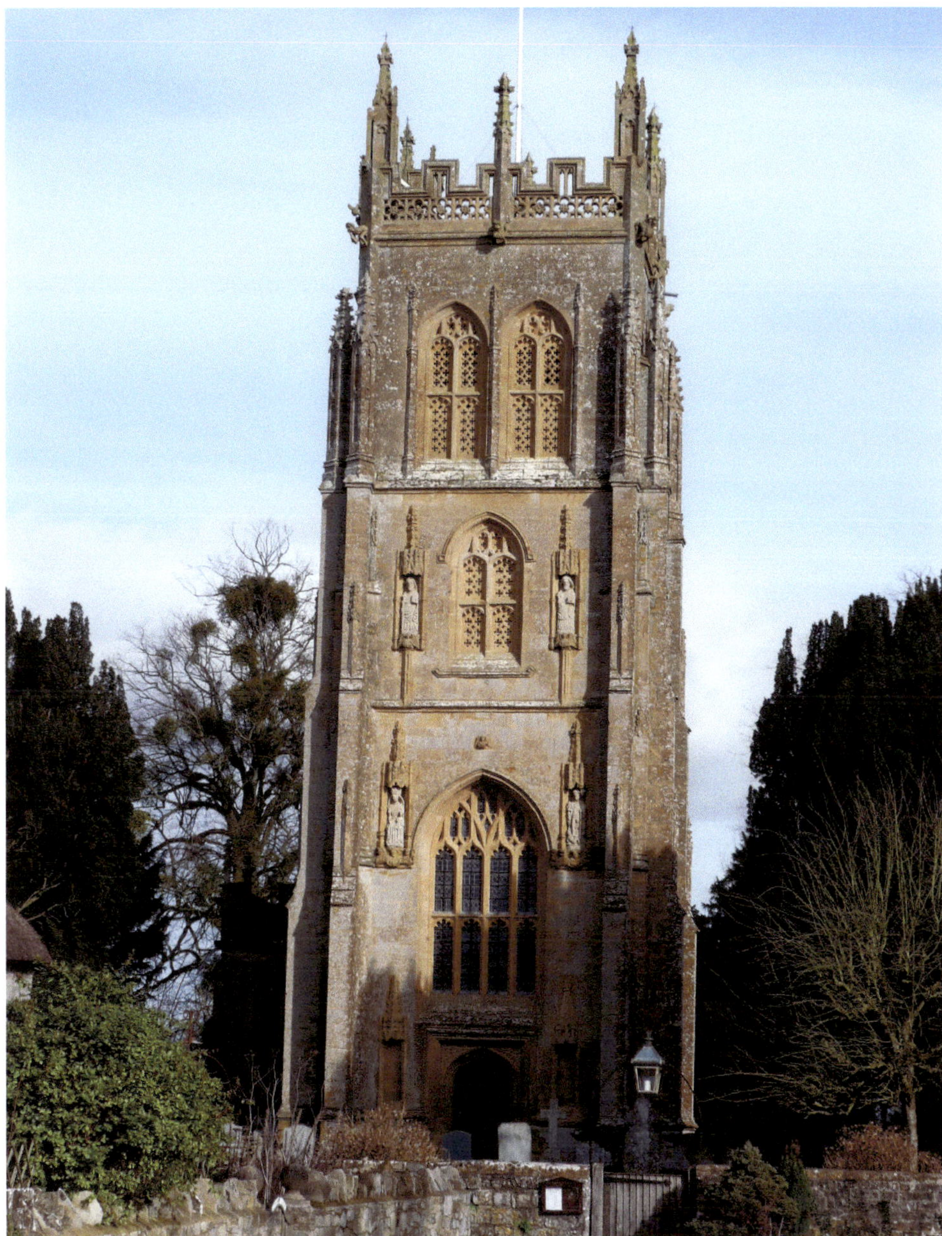

Isle Abbots. Looking at Ham stone but the other three sides are blue lias.

Further hunky punks survive on the north aisle built, like the tower, at the start of the sixteenth century. At the same time, the south porch received an ornate parapet and a fan vault but the outer and inner doorways seem to be late thirteenth-century, like the nave and chancel. The studded door into the church seems to be original. Inside the church is light and airy, due to the absence of stained glass today.

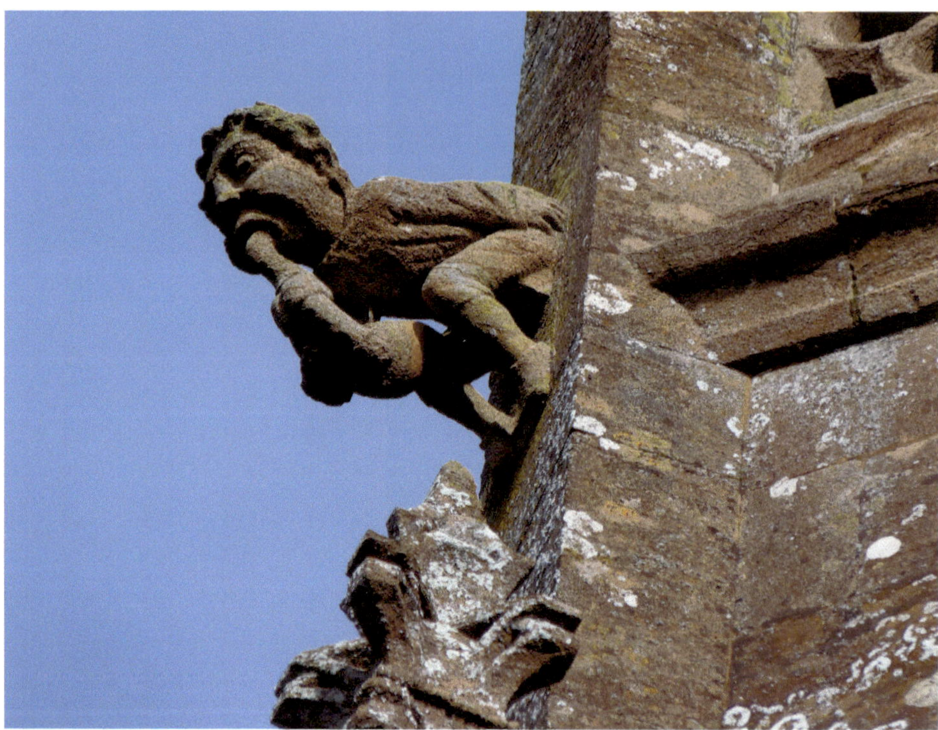

Isle Abbots. Detail from the tower, showing a piper.

The font in the north aisle is Norman, a Ham stone version of what is often seen in Purbeck marble elsewhere. A squint from the aisle to the chancel cuts through the stairs to the former rood loft. The chancel screen is fifteenth-century but missing its lower panels and the cresting and coving. The bench ends are of a similar date but the elegant pulpit is Jacobean. The chancel side windows have early Geometrical tracery but the east window is of five stepped lancets under a single arch. On the south side are two very special features, quite unique and rather sumptuous. A piscina with shelf is set in the centre of a five-bayed panelled design whilst the sedilia to the west are like three tub chairs set against cusped panelled arches, the tops of which have been restored. The church does not contain any monuments but special mention must be made of the huge empty stone sarcophagus in the sanctuary; one can only speculate on the size of the person it was made for!

Nearby Curry Rivel Church has a good display of hunky punks.

26. KINGWESTON, ALL SAINTS

This church stands at the end of a no-through road leading north off the Somerton to Castle Cary road. Kingweston is largely an estate village with several of the buildings built by the Dickinson family in the eighteenth century. They were a Quaker family of merchant traders from Bristol and their mansion stands beside the church. All Saints was completely rebuilt to the designs of C. E. Giles (1851–55)

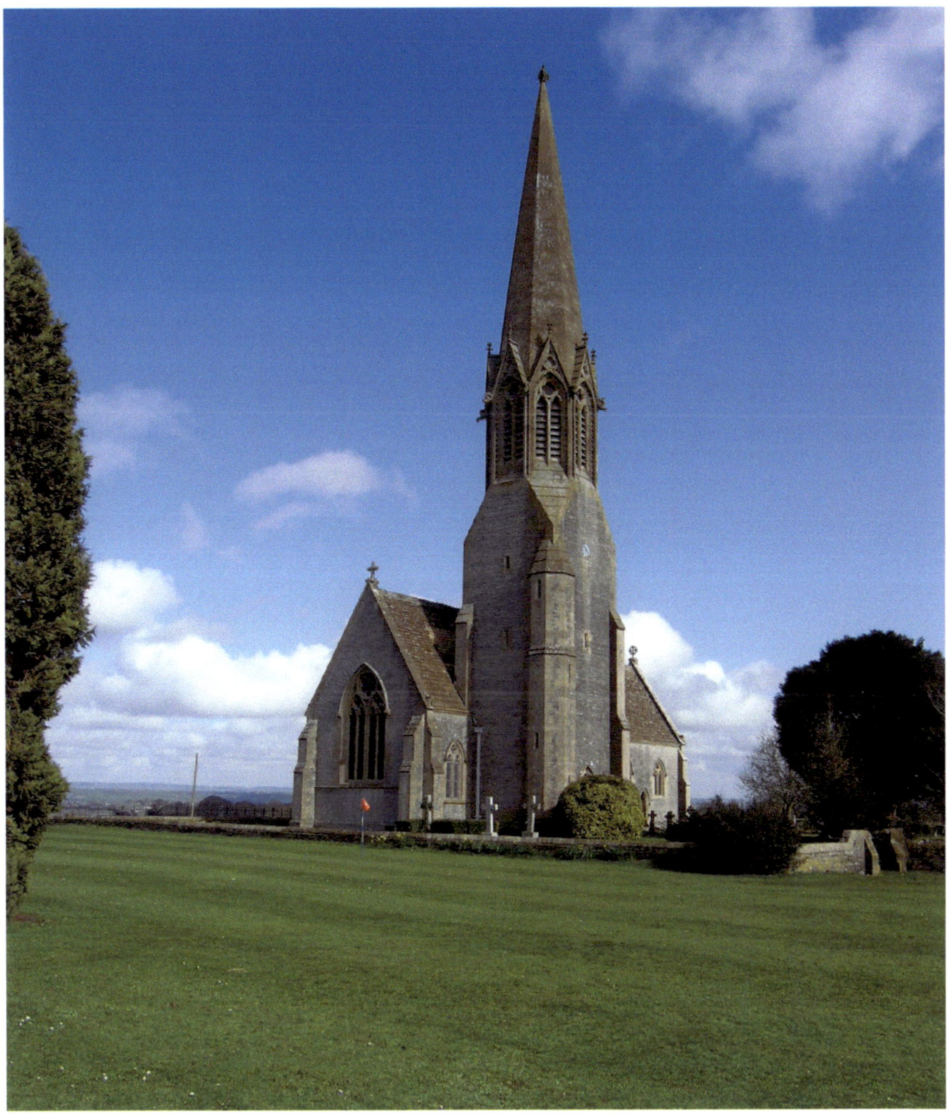

Kingweston. The steeple looks ready for take-off!

for Francis Dickinson and was his first church. Giles went on to work on many other Somerset churches, both restoring them and designing new buildings. The site is medieval as witnessed by the reused Norman doorway under the tower and the twelfth-century font from the former church. The doorway has an inner arch of lattice work with little pellets which is framed by two columns with scalloped capitals carrying two semi-circles of chevron decoration. The present church consists of a nave and chancel but what makes it special is the south porch tower and the exuberant decoration inside the chancel. The steeple looks like a rocket about to launch into space and is quite out of scale with the church itself. The octagonal top

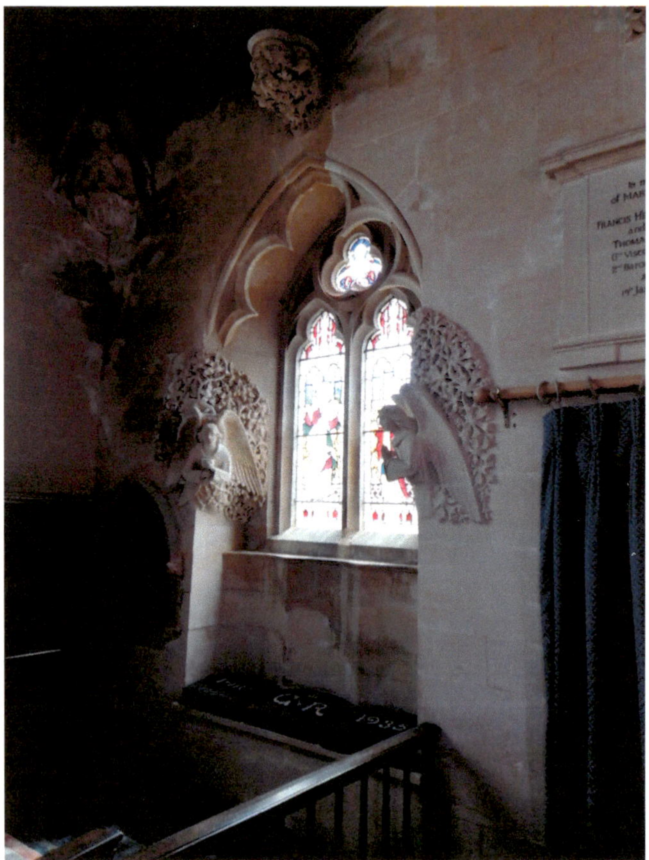

Kingweston. Lush
sculpture in the chancel.

of the tower resembles that of Lostwithiel in Cornwall. The sculptured details in the
chancel are worthy of note with their lush foliage and angels. The south window
is continued down to form a stone seat, but the corners have angels with wings
outstretched across a bed of leaves. A sketch of 1838 at the west end of the nave
shows the previous church.

27. Leigh-on-Mendip, St Giles

The church possesses one of the best towers in a county of fine towers. It is similar
to nearby Mells but even more ornate and out of proportion to the short nave and
the very low chancel. The tower is of four stages and is just over 91 feet 6 inches
high (28m). It fairly bristles in pinnacles, some twenty-eight in total – eight to
the third stage on top of the buttresses and another twenty crowning the top of
the tower. The top stage has three two-light transomed bell openings, the third
stage similar but with blank tracery. The second stage has two niches and a small
window on the south side; the other three sides are blank. It is therefore surprising
after such a display to discover that St Giles was only a chapelry of Mells until
1860. The nave clerestory parapet has two rows of quatrefoils on the south side

and only the upper tier is pierced. The south aisle also has a pierced parapet of quatrefoils. The north side is plainer, and the chancel has plain parapets. The short but lofty nave is emphasised internally by the three-bayed arcades where the west bay is narrower and lower than the other two. Both nave and chancel have impressive tie-beam roofs resting on large stone corbels of angels and with large central bosses on the tie beams with further angels. The nave roof has a ceilure and the ornamentation of the chancel roof is further enriched by vine trails.

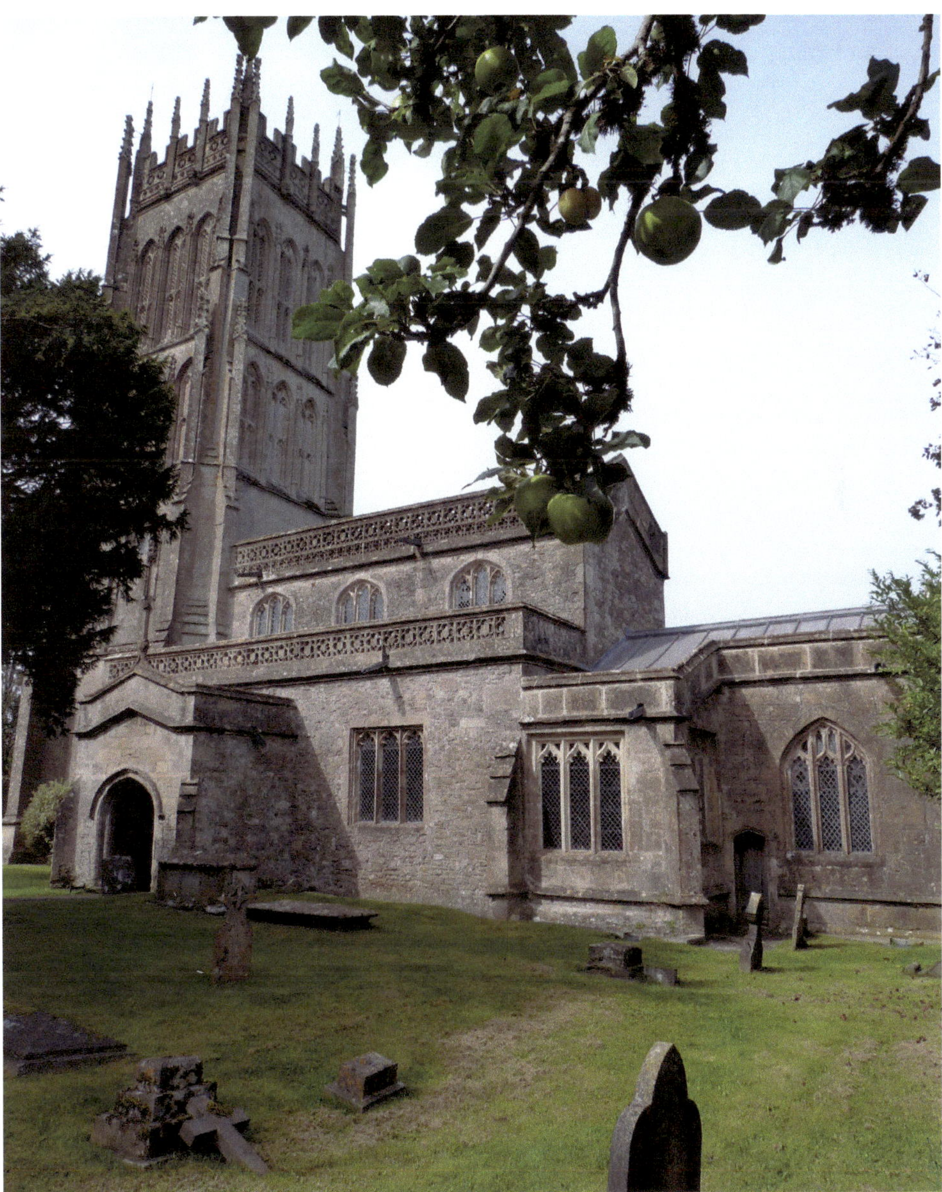

Leigh-on-Mendip. Tall tower, short lofty nave and very low chancel.

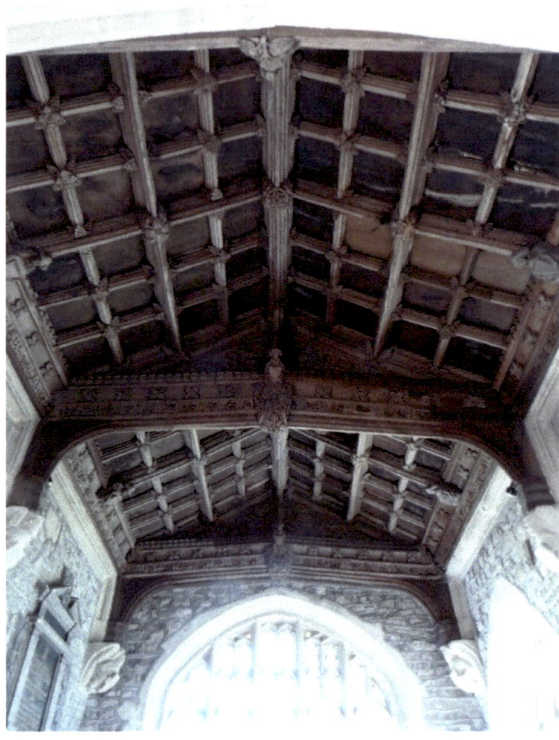

Leigh-on-Mendip. Detail of the chancel roof.

Two stone angel corbels at the sanctuary steps were used to support a Lenten veil. A complete set of late fifteenth-century benches have traceried ends. The font is Norman, square, with scallops under the bowl but the cover is later with a central baluster and supporting stays making it look like a crown. The tower was to have been vaulted (see the springers) and the west window has a collection of medieval stained-glass fragments, some of the roundels with Instruments of the Passion and others with random heads. Finally, under the tower, a nice welcoming area has been provided with display boards and, when not manned, an honesty café. An incident in 1857 saw the minister, who had preached about drunkenness, covered in bull's blood fired from a gun by a member of the congregation who had not liked what he had heard. The unfortunate fellow was sentenced to two years' imprisonment!

28. LOW HAM, DEDICATION UNKNOWN

Known as 'the church in a field', Low Ham is no longer in regular use and is vested in the Churches Conservation Trust. There is no churchyard and indeed the church stands in a field alongside a farmyard. Apart from the broad west tower, the church is a strange Gothic design which tries to match the local style of over 100 years earlier. It was begun in 1620 by Sir Edward Hext and completed by his grandson George Stawell who died in 1669 and whose initials and crest are on the south door of the chancel. The church consists of a short three-bay nave with clerestory, aisles and chancel all with embattled parapets. The window tracery

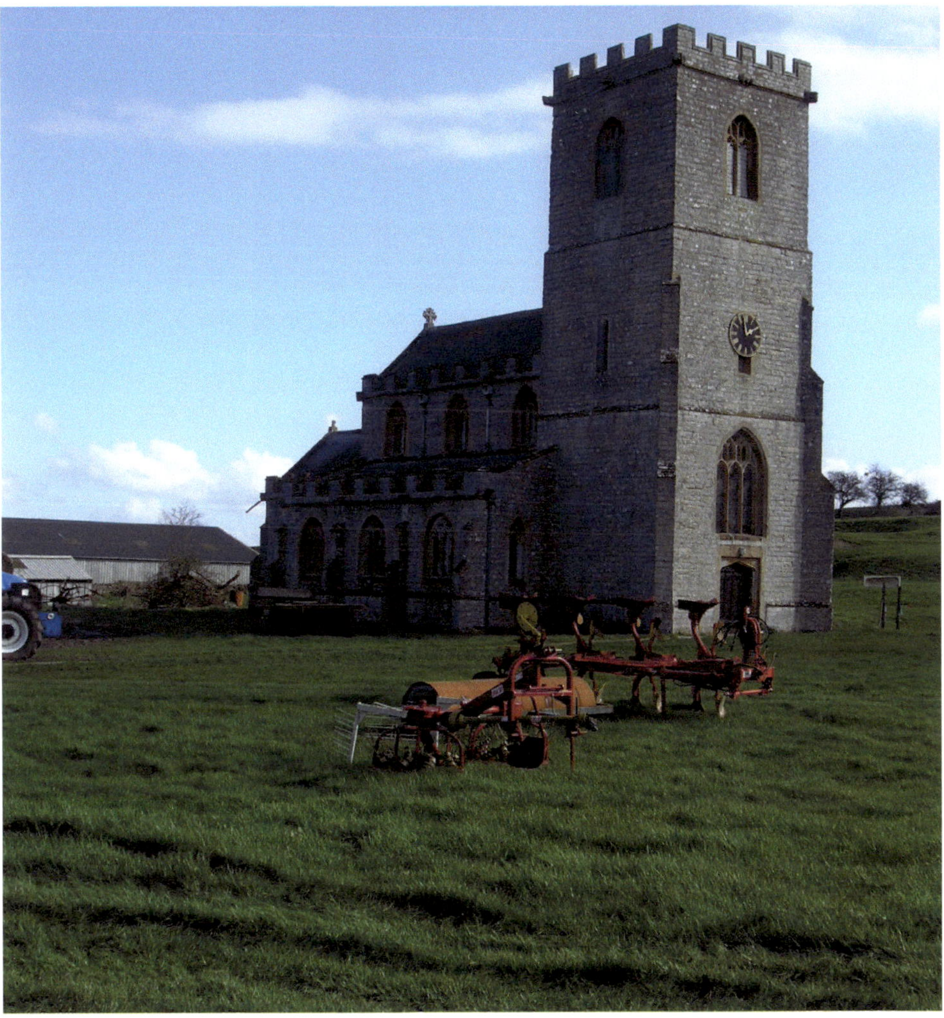

Low Ham. The church in the field.

has no medieval basis and that of the east window is quite memorable. Entry is via the west door where you immediately encounter an ornate Gothic screen of 1823 installed here after 1889 when it was taken out of the Lord Mayor's Chapel in Bristol. It has a large central arch flanked by traceried panels with Georgian stained glass by David Evans, an early pioneer of the revival of the art from Shrewsbury. Another screen to the chancel has the inscription: 'My sonne feare God and the Kinge, and meddle not with them that ar given to change.' This is, like the bench ends, of same period as the church. The pulpit, also seventeenth century, came from nearby Muchelney. Disappointingly, the roofs are Victorian. The glass in the east window dates from *c.* 1690. At the east end of both aisles are family monuments, on the north side a tomb chest with effigies of Sir Edward Hext (d. 1623) and wife (d. 1633), and on the south a stately marble

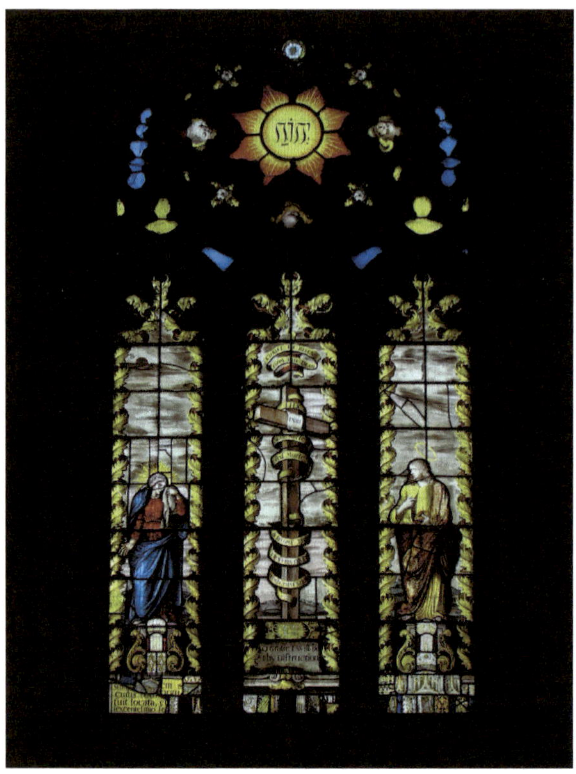

Low Ham. The painted glass of the east window.

standing monument to Ralph, 1st Lord Stawell (d. 1689) and John, 2nd Lord Stawell (d. 1692). The latter began building a large mansion close to the church in 1689 which was never finished and has now completely disappeared.

29. MARTOCK, ALL SAINTS

The church stands at the southern end of this small town. It is Somerset's second largest parish church, all embattled except for the chancel, the tower a little plainer than many others in the county. The chancel is thirteenth century and has a fine east window of five stepped lancets. It is quite long, of four bays, with two-bayed side chapels. The exterior of both chapels bristle with pinnacles; the only others are the four on the tower. Entry is via the south porch which has a stone vault. The interior is broad and spacious with fine six-bayed arcades which have blank squared tracery in the spandrels, a design unique in Somerset but seen in East Anglia (e.g. Lavenham). Above, between the clerestory windows, are elaborate niches, now empty, but painted in the seventeenth century with figures of the Apostles. All of this is a prelude to the magnificent tie-beam roof, dated 1513. Each tie beam is decorated with vine trails and cresting, carries traceried divisions into the roof and has a large central boss with shield-carrying angels. Between each tie beam there are pendant bosses and each bay is profusely panelled. The clerestory is a later addition as witnessed by the former nave roofline above the panelled tower arch and is also the explanation

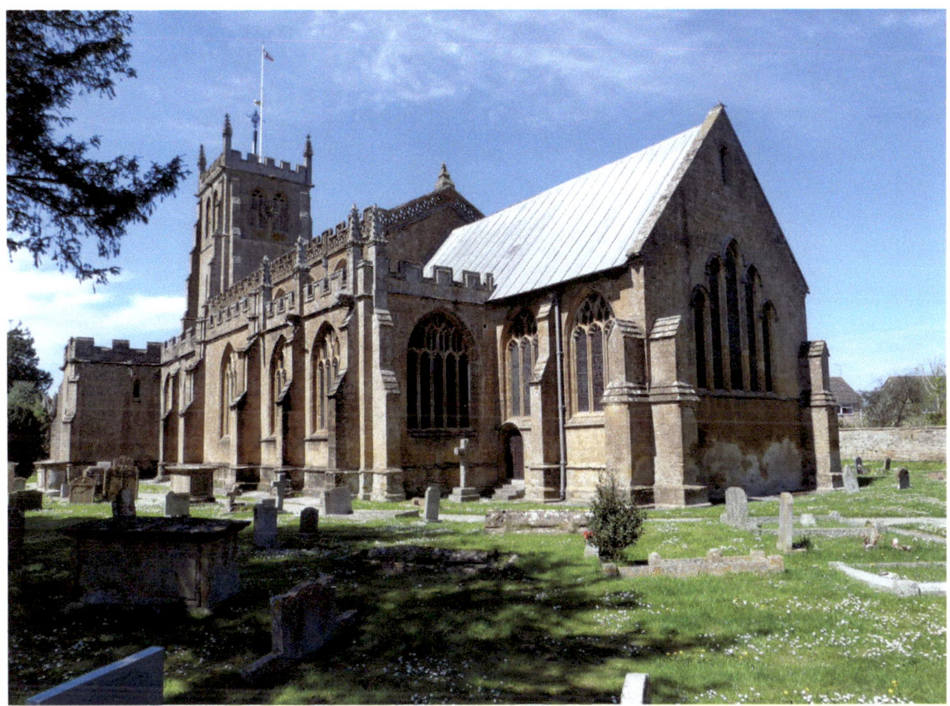

Above: Martock. The impressive exterior from the south-east.

Right: Martock. The nave roof is a superb example of Somerset carpentry.

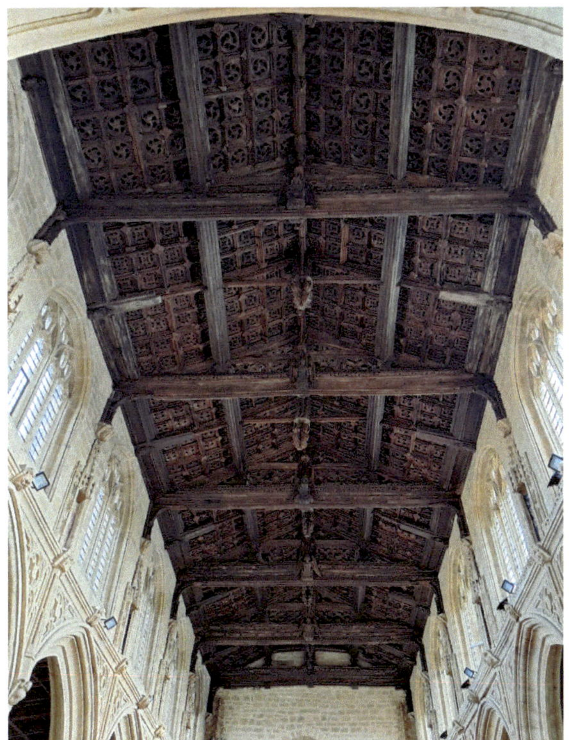

for the beautiful pierced embattled parapet outside. The tower buttresses are brought into the west end of the nave and are embellished by two ornate niches on each side. Apart from the fifteenth-century font, the fittings are mostly Victorian or early twentieth century and the stone pulpit of 1883 is particularly handsome. In a recess in the south aisle is a worn effigy of a lady, the arch decorated with fleurons. Another spectacular roof can be seen at nearby Somerton.

30. MELLS, ST ANDREW

The church is set back from the main street from which tantalising glimpses of the tower can be had. The approach to the churchyard is along New Street, built in the mid fifteenth century by Abbot Selwood of Glastonbury, and the church is of the same period. The proud south porch is the latest part of the church, *c.* 1500,

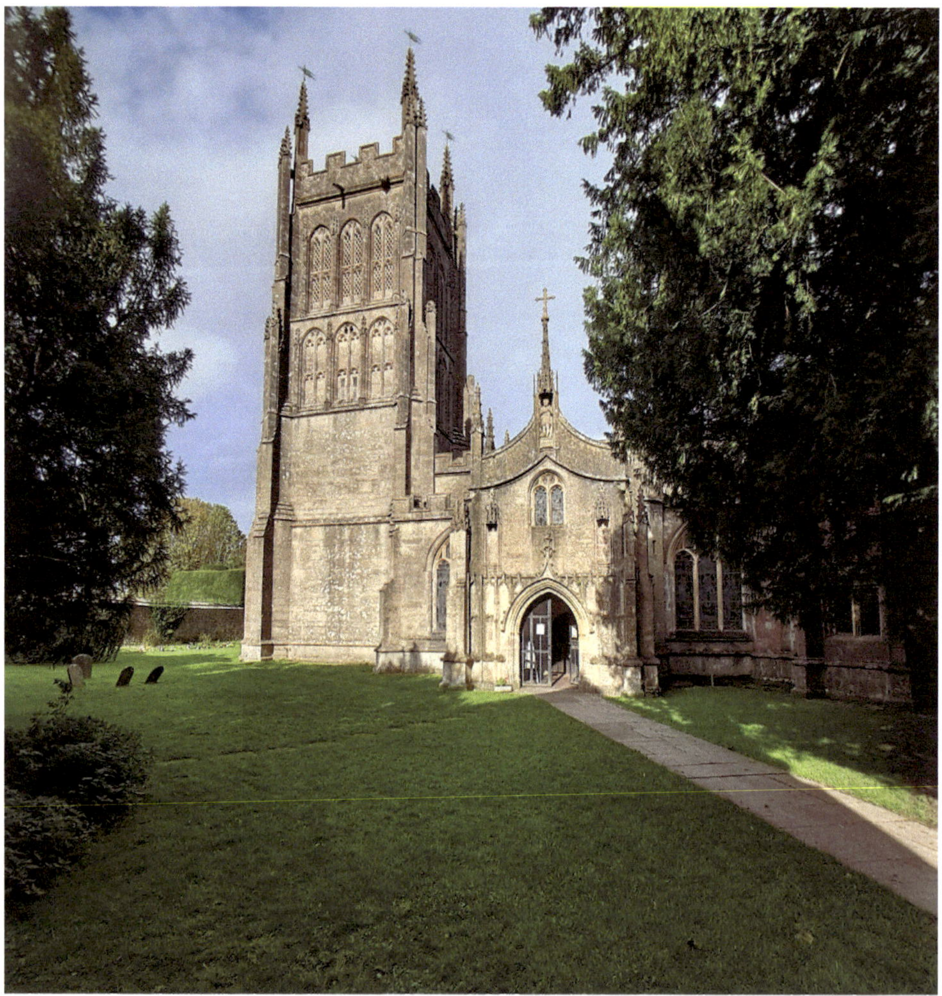

Mells. The peaceful setting for one of the best Somerset towers.

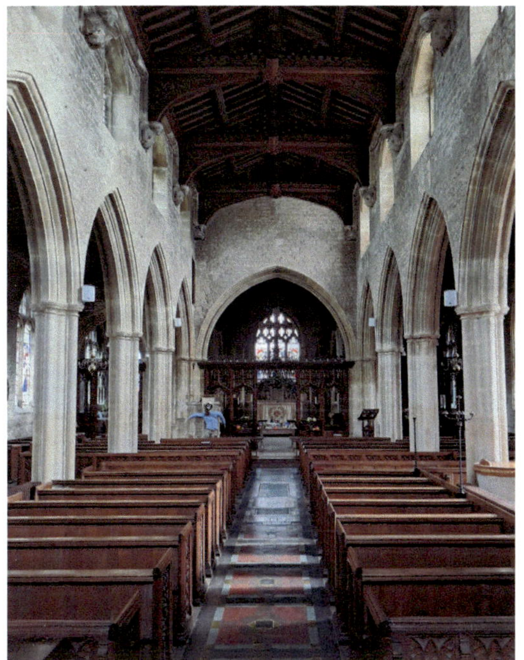

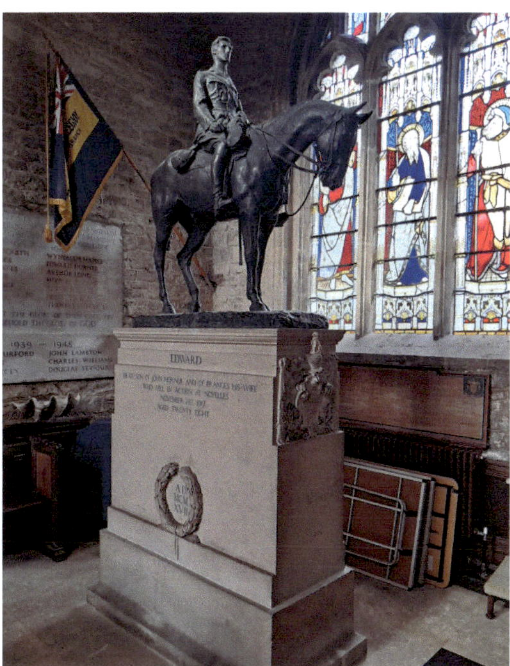

Above left: Mells. The interior was complete with a scarecrow when I visited!

Above right: Mells. The soldier riding his horse in the north aisle.

the ogee hood mould carried up into a pinnacle, the interior with a beautiful fan vault in 2×2 bays around a central panelled rose. There are similar porches at nearby Doulting (also with a near-identical vault) and Wellow. To the east an unusual half-octagonal two-storeyed vestry, 1485, with the arms of the Merchant Taylors' Guild. The west tower is 104 feet high (32m), of four stages, the top two with three two-light transomed windows, blank below and pierced above. The pinnacles surmounting the set-back buttresses are slightly detached from the tower and joined to it by tiny flying buttresses. Inside, the church is fairly standard Perpendicular work with four-bayed arcades and a clerestory, but the roofs are all Victorian replacements. The only surviving feature from the previous church is the cusped thirteenth-century piscina, reset in the chancel. The tower also has a fan vault. The fittings are nearly all of 1880, the gift of the Horner family at the manor house; the polygonal stone pulpit is ornately carved but in contrast the font is a plain Norman tub with a band of cable moulding at the base which is echoed in the font cover. In the north aisle windows are some fifteenth-century stained-glass figures. In the south chapel behind the organ are some Victorian brasses, entirely in the medieval tradition. Visitors may be surprised to see a soldier riding a horse at the west end of the north aisle which was originally in the north chapel and moved here in 2007. It is a memorial to Edward Horner (d. 1917), who died from injuries received in the Battle of Cambrai; the figures are by Sir Alfred Munnings and stand on a plinth by Lutyens, a smaller version of his Cenotaph in

Whitehall, London, all dating from 1920. There is a fine wall memorial designed by Burne-Jones to Laura Lyttelton (d. 1886), a peacock displaying his long tail feathers. At the west end of the south aisle is a framed embroidery depicting the Guardian Angel of Humanity designed by Burne Jones and worked by his friend Lady Frances Horner. Finally, the vestry is panelled with Jacobean bench ends, presumably once in the body of the church. In the churchyard is the simple headstone to Sigfried Sassoon, the wartime poet (d. 1967).

31. NETTLECOMBE, ST MARY

The church stands right next to Nettlecombe Court, a largely Elizabethan mansion which is now a Field Studies Centre. The Trevelyan family removed the village to Woodford in the late eighteenth century to enable the grounds to be landscaped. The church has a fifteenth-century west tower but much else was renewed by C. E. Giles 1858–70, who added the clerestory and rebuilt the chancel arch. The south aisle is earlier than the north aisle but has similar arcades with capitals of bands of foliage, a type more common in Devon. Two windows in the north chapel have medieval glass figures reset in the seventeenth century, but the figure labelled St George is clearly not him. The east window has very pleasant glass by Martin Travers (1935) of the Virgin & Child under a tree and flanked by the court, the church and roundels depicting the four seasons. The benches contain reset

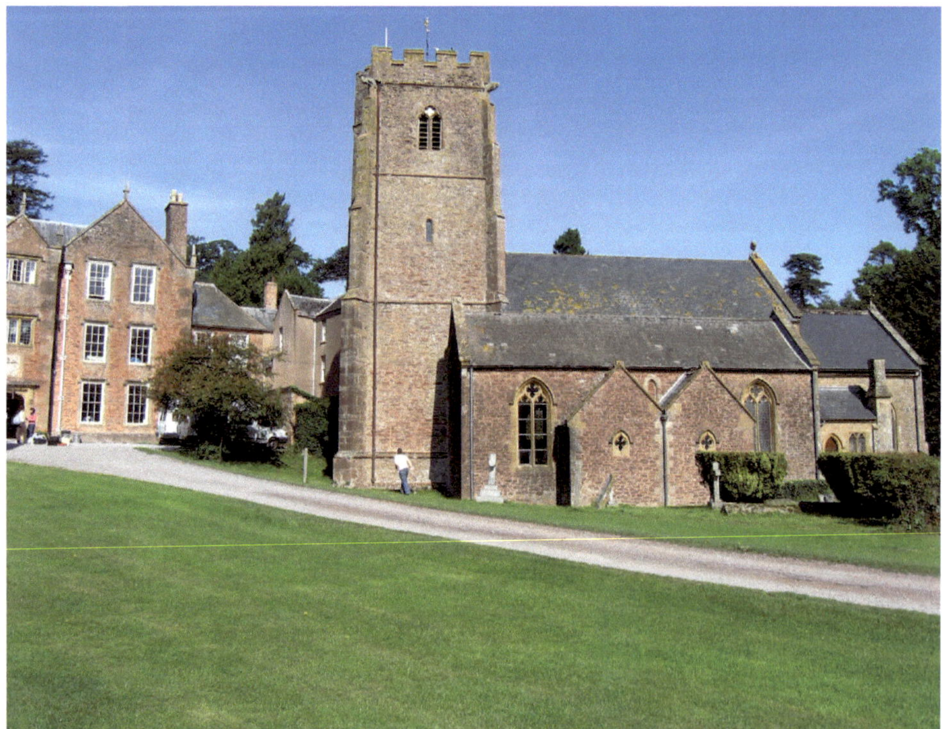

Nettlecombe. The church sits on the lawn of Nettlecombe Court.

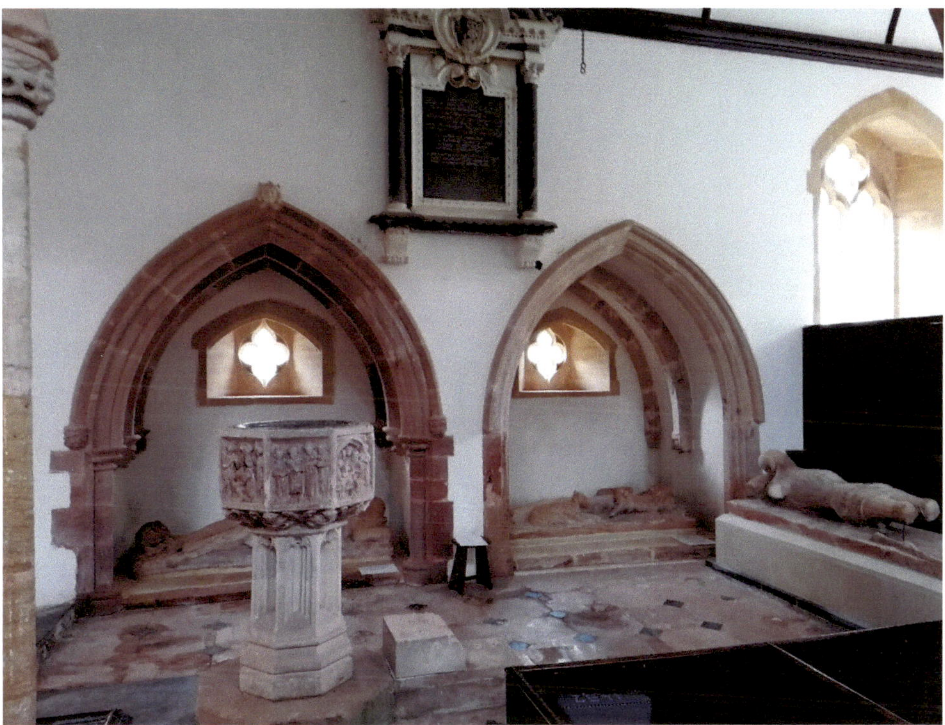

Nettlecombe. The post-2022 arrangement of the monuments and the Seven Sacraments font.

medieval panels as does the tower screen. The pulpit is of *c.* 1700 and is entered using the former rood stairs. In the south aisle stands a fine Seven Sacraments font, one of only two outside of East Anglia. Here too are two fourteenth-century tomb recesses, so deep that they have their own external gables and small windows; they are tunnel-vaulted with stone ribs resting on head corbels. The monuments here were badly affected by damp and poor repairs and were the subject of a ten-year conservation project, completed in 2022. The earliest, in the left-hand recess, is a chainmailed cross-legged knight with a large shield carrying the arms of the Raleigh family. The other recess now only contains a lady and her two dogs, one unusually lying by her side. Her armless and legless partner now lies on a brand-new plinth in the aisle.

32. NORTH CADBURY, ST MICHAEL

The church and the court stand to the south of this village just north of the A303. The tower, tall and quite plain for Somerset, dates from around 1400 and has a tall turret at the south-east angle over the stairs. The church itself was rebuilt shortly afterwards by Lady Elizabeth Botreaux in a large, impressive style and made collegiate in 1427 by appointing seven chaplains and four clerks. This status seems to have been short-lived as the church reverted to a parish church in the early sixteenth century. Apart from a chimney and low fifteenth-century vestry

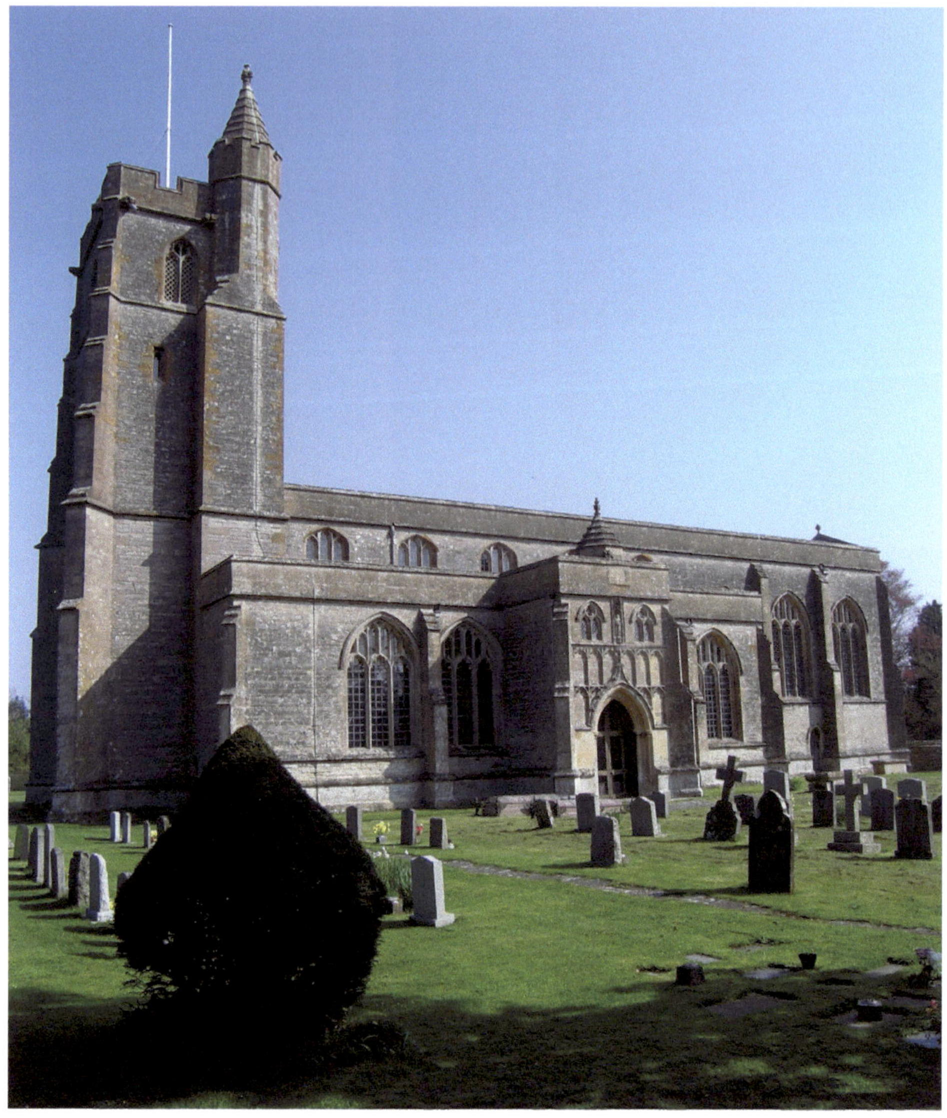

North Cadbury. This south side is almost a mirror image of the north side.

on the north side, the south side of the church is a mirror image. Both porches
have ogee hood moulds which continue up with an image niche flanked by small
two-light windows; blank panelling below and both have vaulting inside. There
are sleek plain parapets to the aisles, porches and to the nave and chancel which is
continuous from the tower to the east end of the chancel. The interior is spacious
with five-bayed arcades, clerestory, and a fine nave roof, dated 1417, with tie
beams and a panelled ceilure. The bench ends are worthy of closer inspection.
Many have amusing heads in profile, including two women nose-to-nose, but also
a flute player, a windmill, a man whipping a horse and a cat with a mousetrap

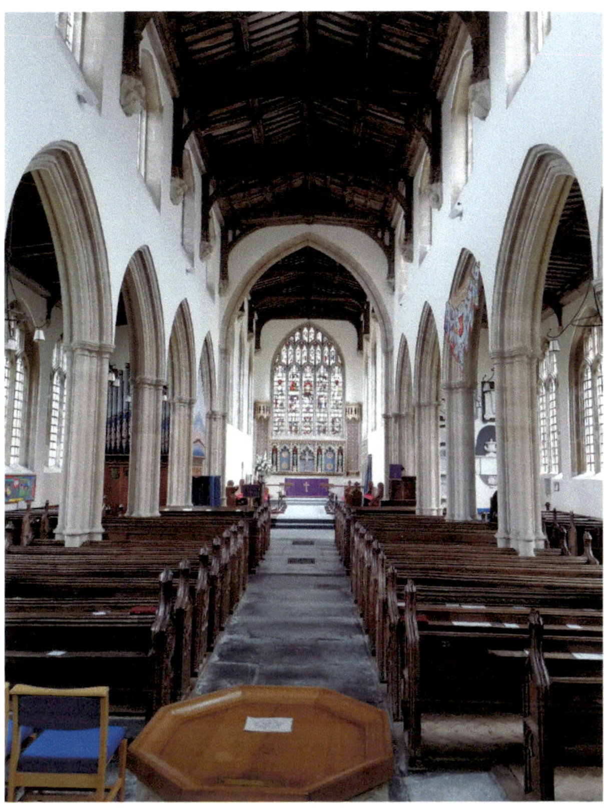

North Cadbury. One of the most perfect interiors in Somerset.

to mention a few. The tomb chest with effigies of the college founder and her husband has been removed from the chancel to under the tower. The chest has standing angels with shields on the long side, a depiction of the Virgin flanked by two donors at the east end and much medieval colour on the west side. Opposite are two large Jacobean tomb chests, likely also re-sited. The chancel has two fine fifteenth-century niches flanking the east window, but the reredos is the work of John Norton. The original figures of the four Evangelists were vandalised and have been replaced by bronze figures by Lyn Constable Maxwell, 2005.

33. NORTH CURRY, ST PETER AND ST PAUL

The church is grouped around an octagonal crossing tower built around 1300, but later additions and alterations have made for a rather awkward appearance outside, especially the nave clerestory where it joins the tower. The former roof pitches were sharper but lower – see the ridge lines that still survive. The parapets are varied, the aisle and north transept are embattled, the south transept has blank arcading, that of the tower is Victorian, and the rest are pierced by quatrefoils and early sixteenth century. The earliest feature is the Norman north doorway. The porch also has an awkward junction with the aisle but is quite showy with three image niches over the outer doorway (statues by Harry Hems, 1881) and

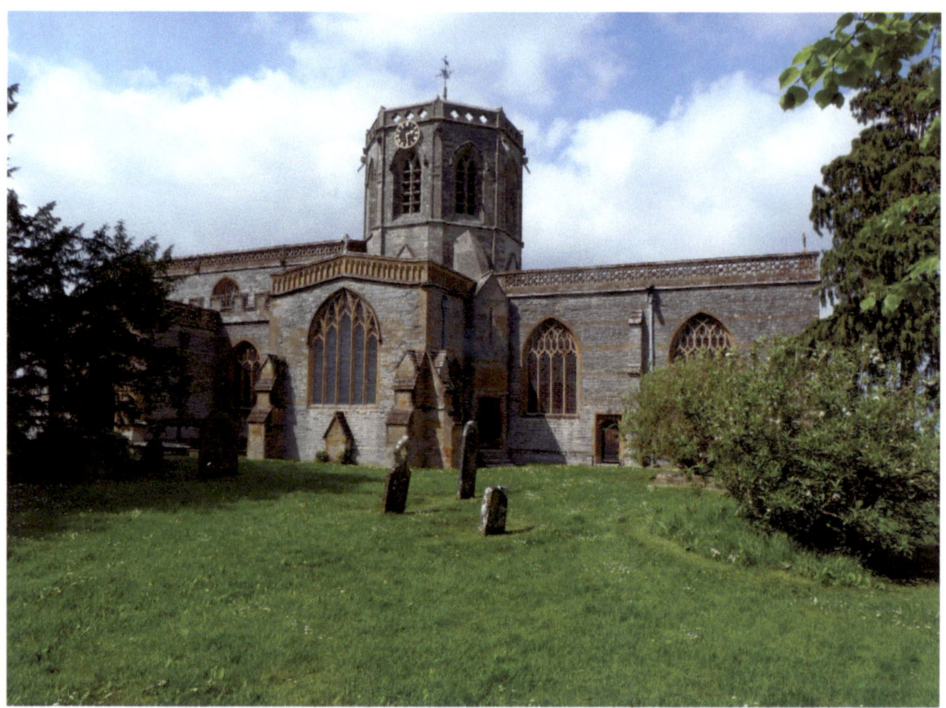

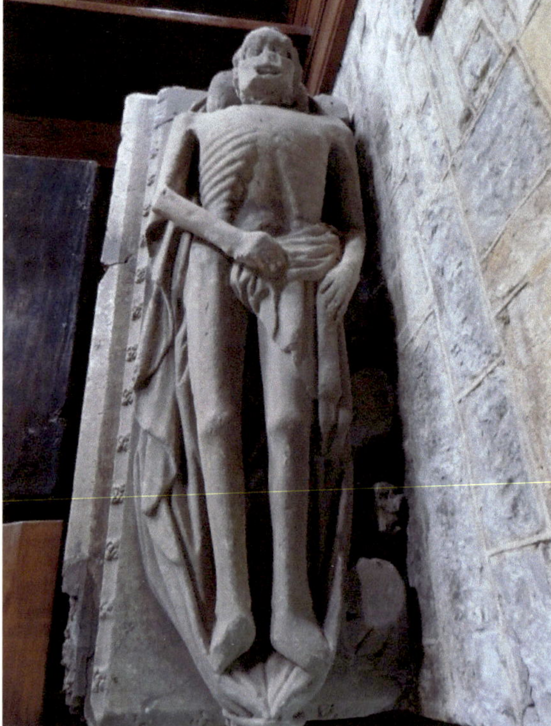

Above: North Curry. The octagonal central tower sits a little awkwardly with later additions.

Left: North Curry. The cadaver effigy in an open shroud in the north aisle.

a fan vault with pendant boss inside. The spacious nave and aisles have arcades without capitals, and on the north side the former clerestory windows have been exposed by the Victorian restorer J. O. Scott. These are out of rhythm with the arches below which match the new clerestory above. The roof is much restored. The crossing arches are triple-chamfered, the eastern arch with band capitals. The wooden fan vault is nineteenth century. Apart from the font, most of the fittings are nineteenth century or early twentieth century. By the west door is an ancient wooden chest with ironwork banding and likely to date back to the twelfth century. The candelabra in the nave dates from 1809. In the chancel is an effigy of a bearded civilian from around 1360 and named in a fold of his gown as Toma of Sloo. In the north aisle a later tomb chest with small figures of mourners and a cadaver effigy on top in an open shroud, similar to that of Bishop Beckington in Wells Cathedral.

Polygonal towers are quite a local feature. South Petherton, Somerton, Barton St David and Stoke St Michael have them.

34. NORTON-SUB-HAMDON, ST MARY

The usual approach to this church passes by a circular dovecote, medieval with buttresses and a conical roof, repaired in the eighteenth century and likely the odd openwork 'hat' dates from this period. The church is Perpendicular, a unified design, and all built in the last part of the fifteenth century. The west tower

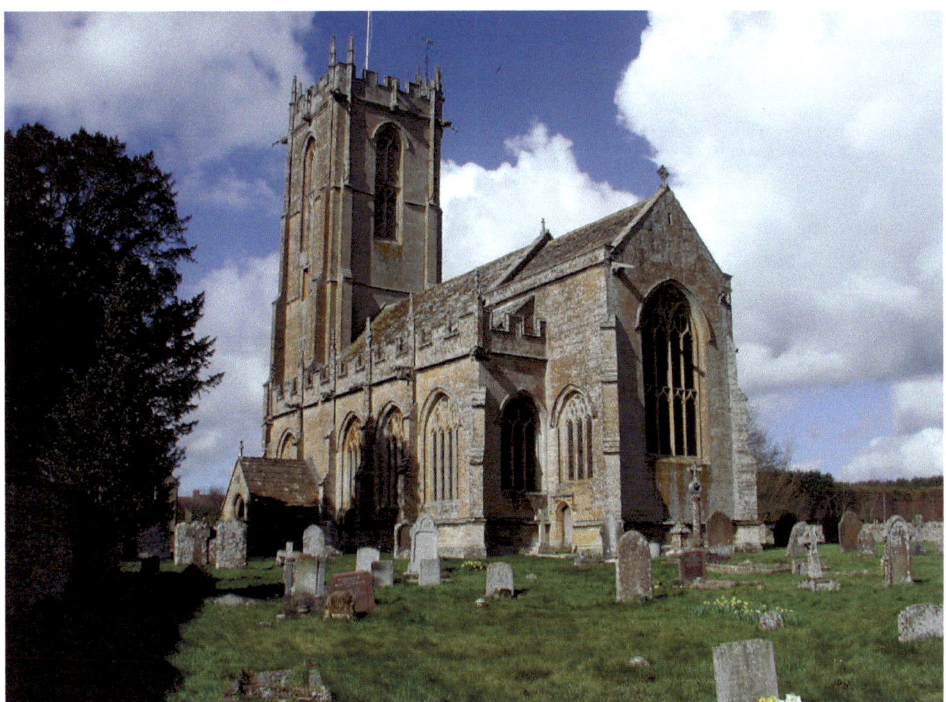

Norton-sub-Hamdon. A singular build of *c.* 1480–1500 of impressive height.

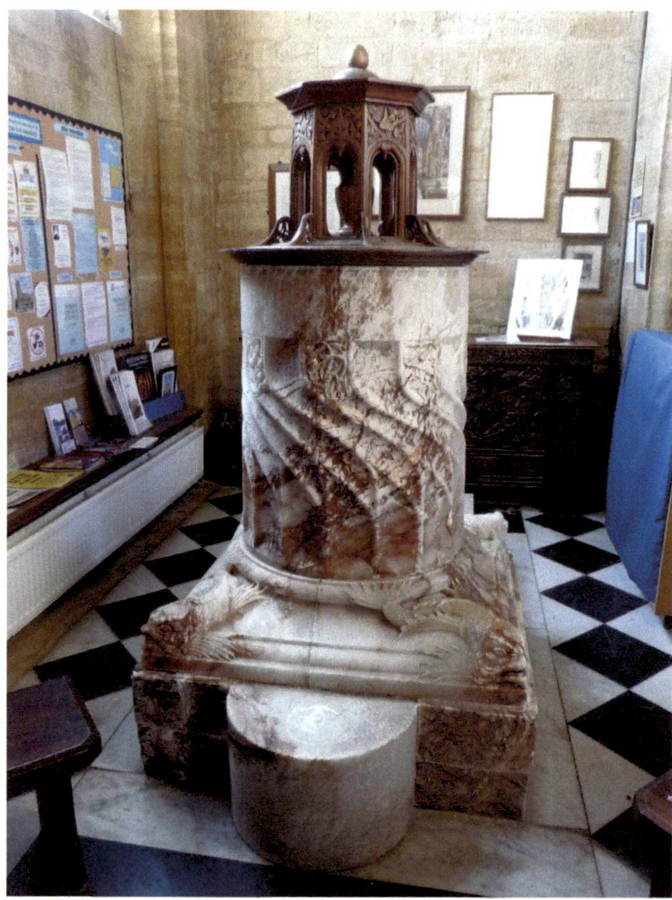

Norton-sub-Hamdon.
The unexpected
Arts & Crafts font by
Henry Wilson, 1894.

resembles the towers at Crewkerne and Hinton St George with long two-light openings through the top two stages. There are set-back buttresses each continuing up through the embattled parapet and topped by pinnacles. The north-east stair turret is a little taller and has its own parapet and pinnacles. The nave and aisles are under one overall roof, the aisles embracing the first bay of the two-bayed chancel with its higher parapet. The loftiness is emphasised when viewed from the south-east and the church greatly resembles Cannington north of Bridgwater. The porch with its cross-ribbed barrel vault must be reused as it does not fit in the aisle bay and has a buttress intruding to the left of the doorway inside. The tower was burnt out and lost its bells following a lightning strike in 1894. The tower was restored by Henry Wilson, who also provided the Arts & Crafts tower screen and the new font in the same style. The latter is a tall, tapered cylinder of pink alabaster with spiral decoration resembling swaves. The base has four fish with spikey fins at the corners. A little earlier is the fine metal screen to the chancel, placed under a very tall chancel arch. The loftiness of the interior is noteworthy, perhaps helped by the blank wall above the tall arcades where you might have expected to see a clerestory.

35. ORCHARDLEIGH, ST MARY

In the grounds of Orchardleigh House and reached from the main road through the estate (helpfully signed) by dropping down through the golf course. There is parking near the church which stands on a small island in a lake linked to the shore by a bridge. The church is late thirteenth century in date, with a large north extension of *c.* 1800. The interior is very dark. Opposite the entrance is an early fourteenth-century canopied tomb recess, now serving as the arch to the family chapel. Any effigy has not survived. There is some unusually rich detailing in the chancel including an aumbry and piscina, two corbels for the Lenten veil and two pedestals for statues (since destroyed), with figures of a king (to the north) with pages tying back his hair and queen (south) with a page and a dog doing the same for her. The aumbry has its original door and above it a figure of Christ triumphing over death (a skull) and two censing angels. Nearly every window has medieval glass reset by Clayton & Bell in 1879. A window is inserted above the priest's door, and in the elongated trefoil is a rare depiction of the Trinity. The font, also *c.* 1300, has a band of foliage springing from the mouths of 'green men' interrupted by medallions with small seated figures. Outside to the south of the church is an impressive monument with a classical urn decorated with swags and animal skulls. It was re-sited here from the parkland in 1989 and is not to a person but to a dog, Azor. He was the devoted pet of Sir Thomas Champneys and died in 1796. He is believed to have been buried in the family vault where his master joined him in 1821. Alongside the church, by the lake, stood the original manor

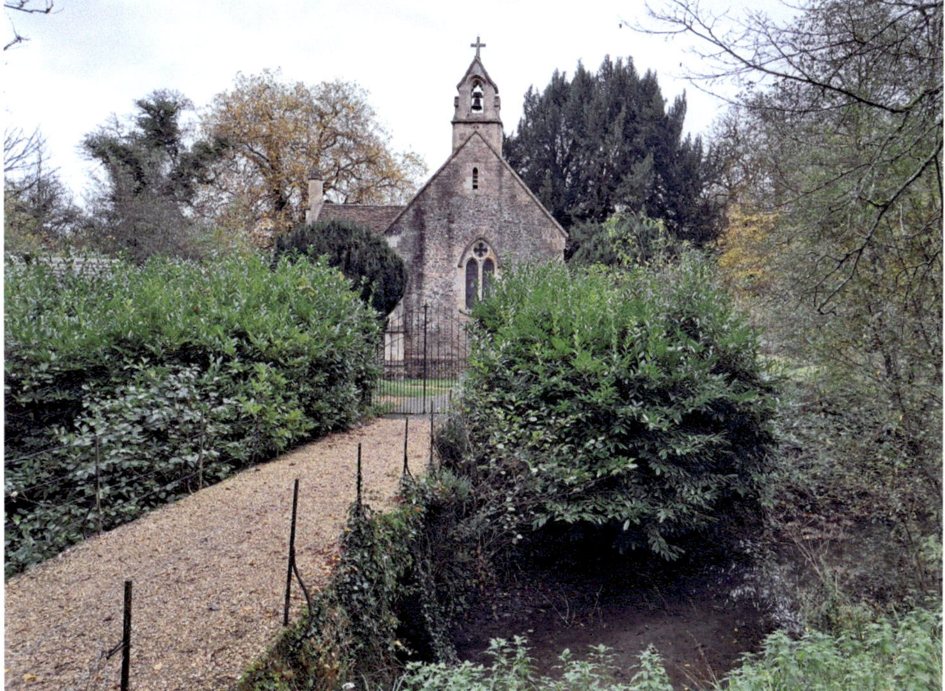

Orchardleigh. The approach over the lake.

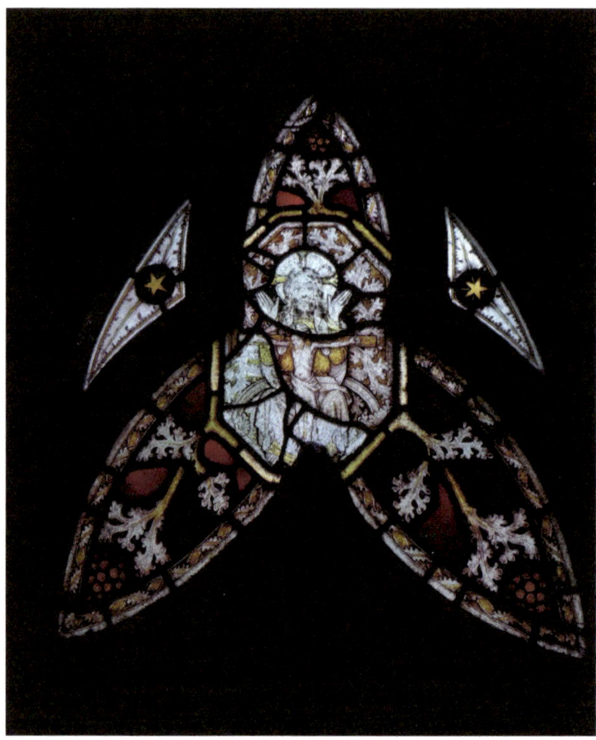

Orchardleigh. Medieval glass of the Trinity in the traceried head of the priest's door.

house but this was demolished in 1860 when the large chateaux-like mansion was built on the hill above. There is much to enjoy here but the setting of the church will live longest in the memory.

36. PUXTON, HOLY SAVIOUR

There are a number of things that you will be able to recall after a visit to Puxton, but it won't be amazing architecture! The church is low-lying, on the edge of Puxton Moor. The first thing you see as you approach from the road is the leaning tower: fifteenth century, not tall, and with a parapet pierced with quatrefoils. The parapet on the south side has been rebuilt without piercings, maybe when the pyramidal roof, dated 1773, was built. The nave may be twelfth century, but the windows are fourteenth and fifteenth century. The roof was lowered in the sixteenth century. The porch carries a coat of arms of the St Loe family and the date '1557' over the entrance. The chancel was rebuilt in 1884–85. The main feature inside is the largely unrestored nave and its fittings: plain benches, probably sixteenth century, Jacobean pulpit and reading desk both seventeenth-century and late eighteenth-century box pews. Earlier is the Norman stone font which has a seventeenth-century cover. The royal arms on the north wall were painted in Banwell in 1775 and on the west wall are boards with the Commandments, Lord's Prayer and Creed, one dated 1825; a benefactors' board is placed on the east wall. There is a low stone screen to

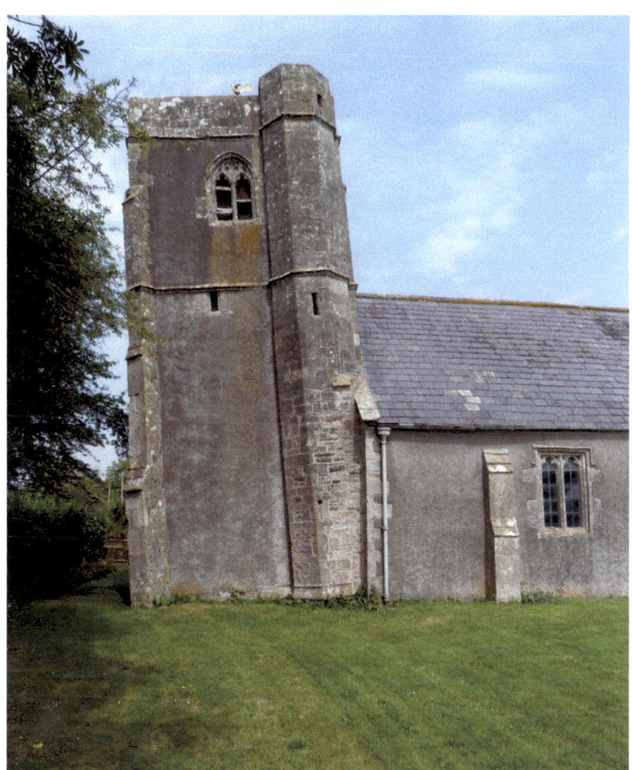

Right: Puxton. The leaning tower from the south.

Below: Puxton. The unrestored interior looking west.

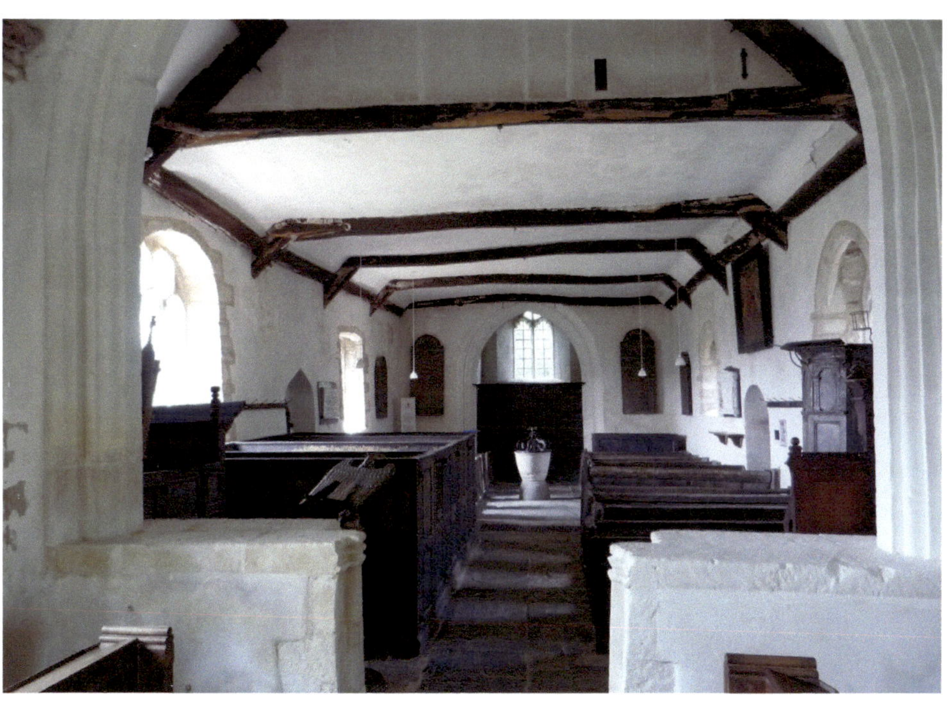

                    Churches of Somerset

the chancel, likely built in the fifteenth century, but the chancel furniture was replaced in the 1880s except for the Jacobean altar rails. The church closed in 2002 and is vested in the Churches Conservation Trust. The leaning tower and the unrestored interior are what you will recall at home after a visit here.

37. RODNEY STOKE, ST LEONARD

The church stands at the southern end of the village and has a simple unassuming exterior with west tower, a nave with pretty openwork parapet and pinnacles, a north porch and a chancel with north chapel and Victorian vestry and organ chamber. On entering, the interior is also simple and, walking down the nave, first the seventeenth-century woodwork is evident including the pulpit and the chancel screen of 1625. The chancel north wall has two fine monuments, the first to Sir Thomas Rodney (d. 1471) which is open to the north chapel and has a recumbent effigy in armour and big canopy above, the second appears to have reused an Easter Sepulchre and has no figures but under its Tudor arch a row of three shields in panels. In the north chapel are three more monuments of great interest, which are to other members of the Rodney family. Under the east window is a beautiful alabaster effigy of Anne Lakes (d. 1630) under an arch and the detailing of her clothes and hair are exquisite. Her nephew George Rodney (d. 1651) is placed on the south wall and shows the young man (aged 21) rising from his coffin. He was only direct heir to his father's estate but died before his

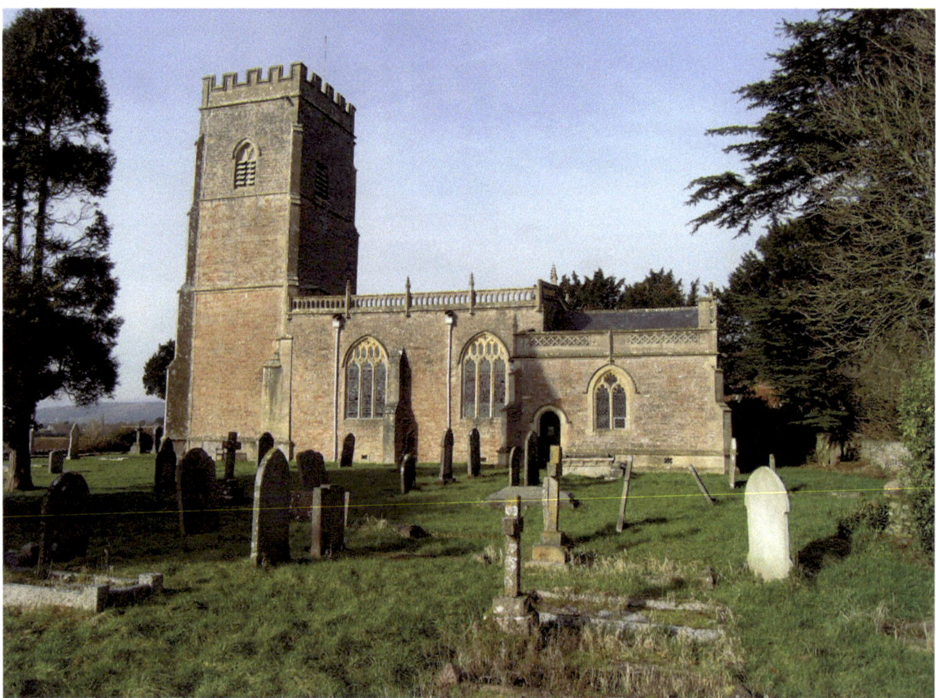

Rodney Stoke. The unassuming exterior from the south.

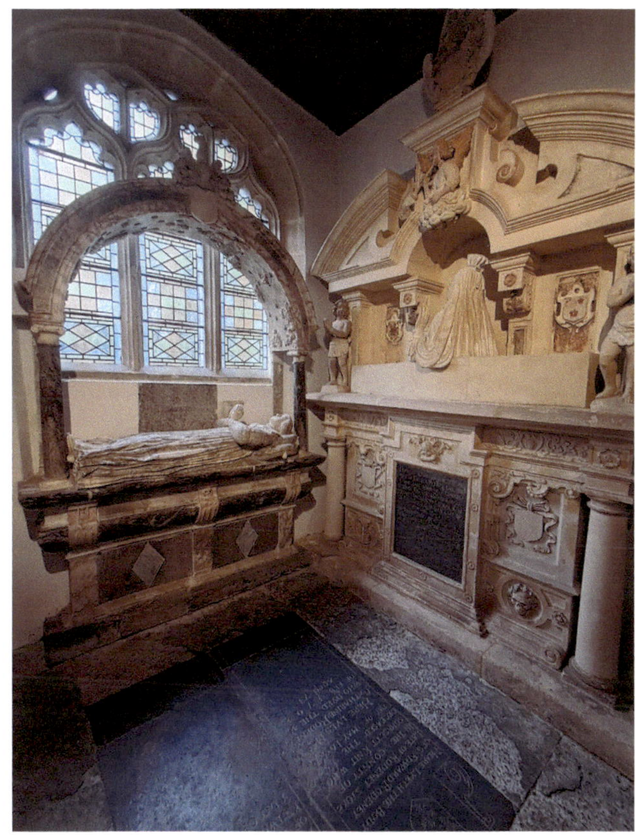

Rodney Stoke. Two of
the Rodney monuments,
including George rising from
his coffin.

father whose monument is on the west wall of the chapel; Sir Edward Rodney
(d. 1657) and his wife are depicted with busts placed in oval recesses. Before
leaving the church note the window opposite the door which commemorates the
safe return of all the people who left the village during the First World War. This
makes Rodney Stoke a 'Thankful Village', one of nine in Somerset and one of only
fifty-three in England and Wales.

38. SELWORTHY, ALL SAINTS

The picturesque village of Selworthy lies north of the A39 on the side of a hill and
the white-painted church is visible from afar. Many visitors each year are drawn
here by thatched cottages and tearoom belonging to the National Trust and the
church benefits greatly from this influx of people. The lower parts of the church
tower are fourteenth century, but the rest is fifteenth century. A splendid south
aisle was added in 1538 (see the date on a capital of the arcade), with its large
transomed windows, the transom embellished by a row of tiny quatrefoils in the
spandrels of the cusped lights below. The roof of this aisle is a feat of carpentry,
the wall plates decorated with seventeen angels holding shields, a feature also
found at Watchet. Most of the other roofs are Victorian. The aisle was likely built

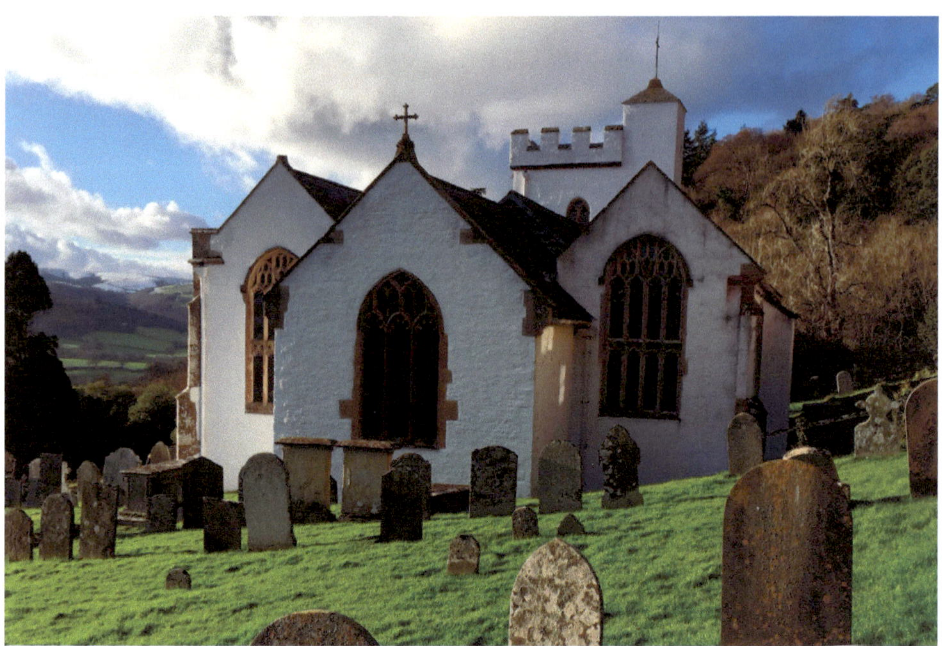

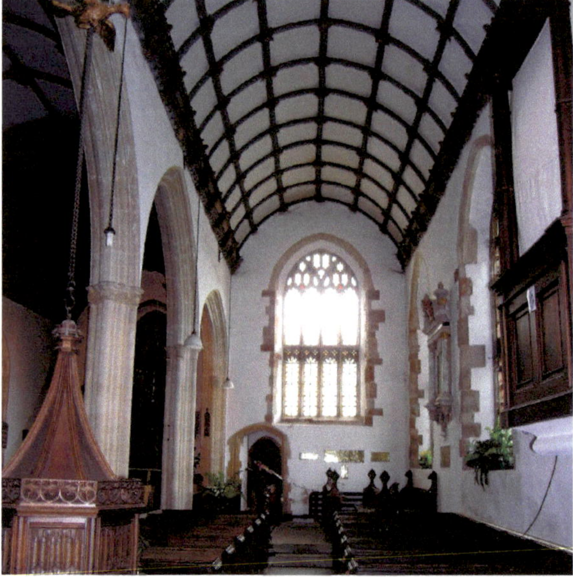

Above: Selworthy. The whitened exterior and the distant hills of Exmoor. (Photo by William Newsom)

Left: Selworthy. The interior of the south aisle.

by the Steynings family of the Holnicote estate which passed to the Acland family and they opened up the room over the porch into the church by a pavillion of 1804 when this became their family pew, looking more like a box at the opera. Earlier is the bulky west gallery of 1750 and earlier still the elegant pulpit of the early sixteenth century with later tester (seventeenth century) above and an hourglass for time-limiting the sermons. The font is Norman but reworked and it is shaped rather like a thistle. The font cover is as big as the font with linenfold panels and cresting and a short panelled spire. It dates from 1930. There is a Perpendicular table tomb in the chancel and two hanging monuments of the early eighteenth century in the south aisle, one having a panel with three cherub heads below the inscription. At the west end are two near-identical monuments, both by Sir Frances Chantrey to three members of the Dyke-Acland family with profile portrait medallions. One is to two brothers; the older died in his mid-twenties of 'African fever' whilst on naval service and was buried on the island of Ascension. His parents heard of his death two months afterwards and within a few weeks his youngest sibling also died aged ten. The monument records that he was a good little boy, early ripened for Heaven. Finally, closing the linenfold panelled door behind you on leaving, there cannot be many better views to be had from a church porch in the country.

39. STOGURSEY, ST ANDREW

The church at Stogursey (or Stoke Courcy) stands at the east end of the main street. It is a large and somewhat foreboding cruciform church with a rectangular central tower that has a recessed copper-clad spire. The crossing and transepts date from around 1100 and the church was a Benedictine priory belonging to Lonlay Abbey in Normandy, France. The priory was suppressed along with all other so-called alien monastic foundations in 1414. The chancel and side chapels were rebuilt in

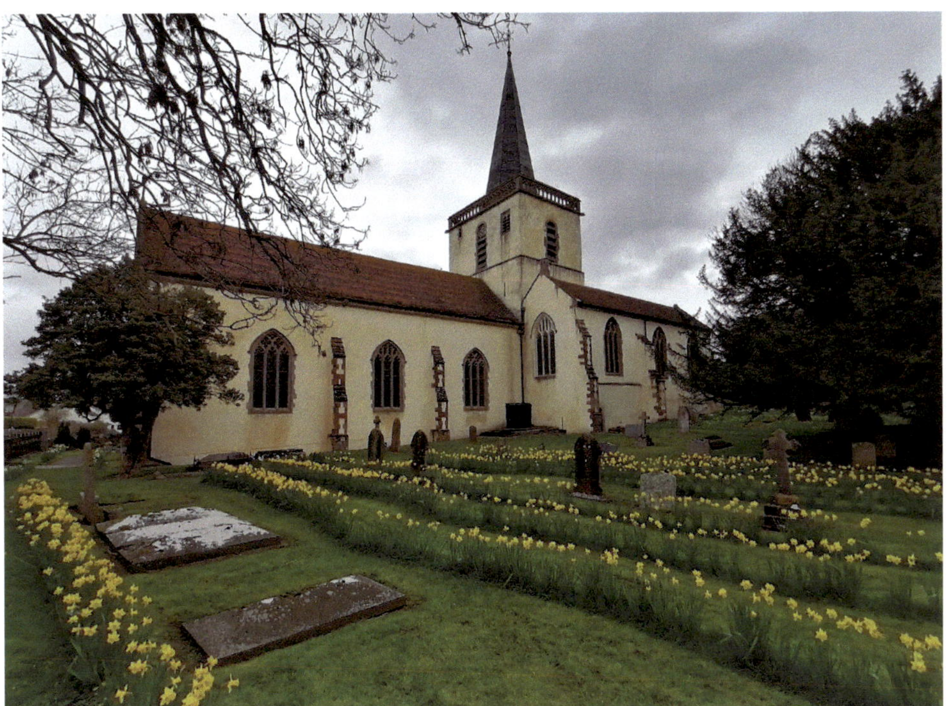

Stogursey. The springtime exterior showing the odd rectangular central tower.

around 1180 and are late Norman, but the neo-Norman east end is the work of John Norton who restored the church in 1862–63. He also added the openwork parapet to the tower. The nave was rebuilt *c.* 1500 in a simple Perpendicular style without aisles and with a reset Norman west doorway. The angel roof inside is Victorian although a few of the angels are medieval. The bench ends here have the beginnings of Renaissance features and have plants, tracery and several birds including a spoonbill with an eel in its mouth; don't miss the man in a loincloth seemingly dancing while holding up a large branch. The crossing has impressive arches resting on capitals which have a variety of foliage decoration including a green man and various odd-looking animals. The two-bayed arcades to the chancel chapels are late Norman and have decoration similar to that found at the Lady Chapel at Glastonbury Abbey. The columns stand on high bases which suggests that the chancel was raised up many more steps than now as found on the Continent. There are also two large Norman fonts, one brought here from nearby Lilstock. There is an impressive collection of monuments in the south chapel. There are two tomb chests. One is very plain and has the effigy of William de Verney (d. 1333) holding his heart, which was buried here whilst his body was interred at Hillfarrance, south-west of Taunton. The second tomb chest carries the fine effigy of John de Verney (d. 1461) in armour. The chest is decorated with six figures in shallow niches on the long sides and a queen and St John on the short sides. Two early eighteenth-century standing monuments with finely sculpted cherubs, including two standing by an obelisk decorated with flowers.

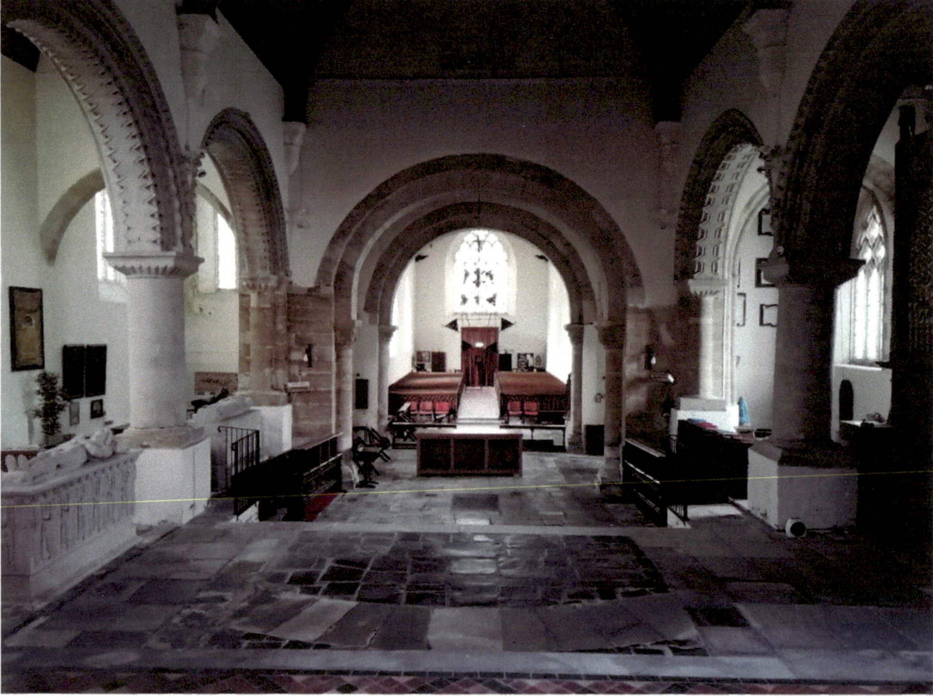

Stogursey. The interior looking west from the chancel.

Set in the floor in the north transept is an ichthyosaur fossil placed here in 1944. An odd, twisted column surmounted by a cube was given to mark the twinning of Stogursey and Lonlay l'Abbaye in 1986. It is a screw from an old cider press and the cube bears the coat of arms of Lonlay and the medieval seal of Stoke Courcy.

40. TAUNTON, ST MARY MAGDALEN

There are three tall church towers in the centre of the county town, this (the tallest) St James (also medieval) and St George (Victorian, the main Catholic church today). The approach along the Georgian Hammet Street is most memorable and the full extent of the 165-foot (50m) tower can be enjoyed. It dates from the last years of the fifteenth and early sixteenth centuries but was taken down and faithfully rebuilt 1858–62 by Benjamin Ferrey and George Gilbert Scott. It is built from red sandstone with Ham stone dressings. There are four stages

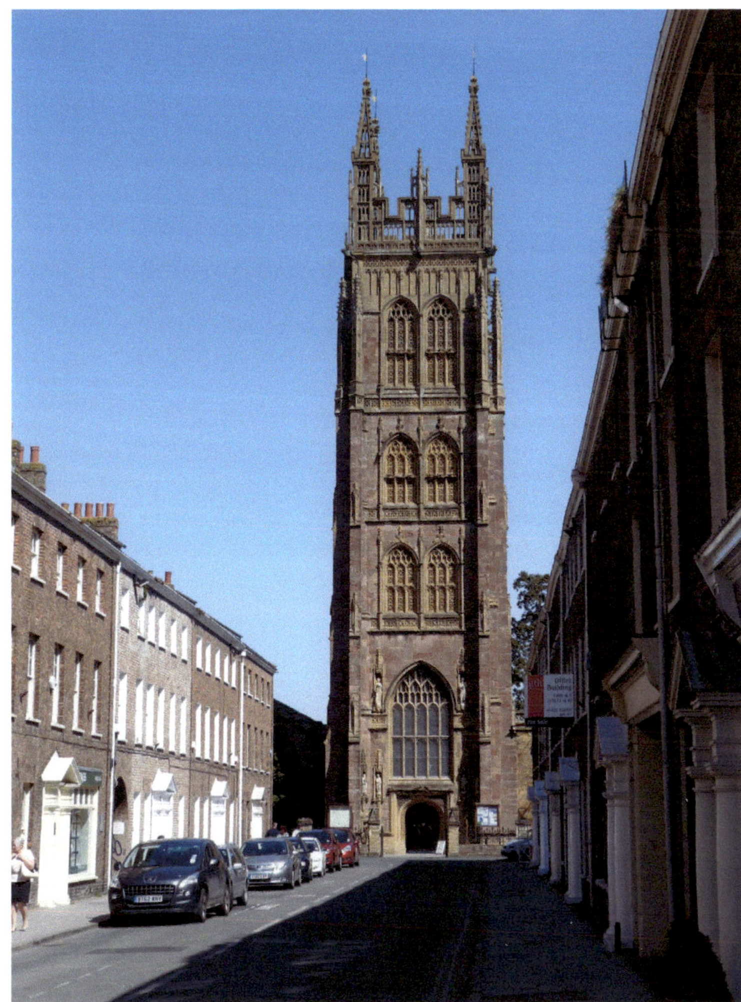

Taunton, St Mary Magdalen. The fine tower closes off the end of Hammett Street.

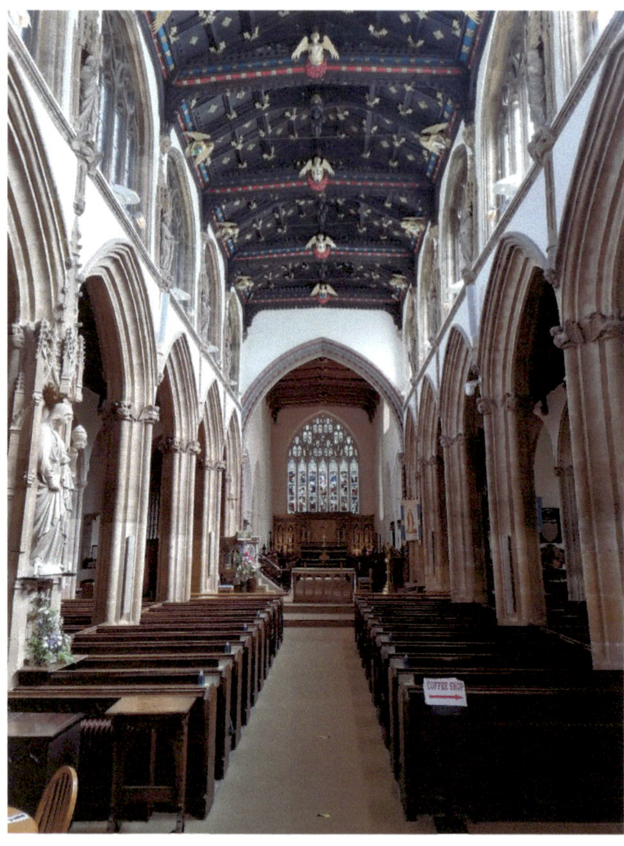

Taunton, St Mary Magdalen. The details of the nave roof are picked out in gold leaf.

with pairs of three-light windows with transom, blank to the middle two stages and pierced and a little taller for the bell stage. The set-back buttresses continue upwards as detached pinnacles linked by tiny flying buttresses to the top stage of the tower. All is finished off by a crown, an embattled pierced parapet and corner openwork pinnacles, a style which spread south-westwards from Gloucester to Bristol (St Stephen), Dundry and Glastonbury from the mid-fifteenth century onwards. The rest of the church appears all Perpendicular, the south side with the fine two-storeyed vaulted porch – showier than the plain north side. The main entrance today is via the west door; note the spandrels of this doorway with two scenes from the legend of the Magdalene. Inside, the tower has a panelled arch and a fan vault. There are four six-bayed arcades as there are double aisles, not really noticeable from outside. The arcade between the two north aisles is the only earlier feature, late thirteenth-century. In the nave there are niches between the clerestory windows and also a large elaborate niche on the north arcade, all with Victorian statues. The nave roof is spectacular, with tie beams, panelling with little gilded flowers and gilded angels. Most of the fittings are Victorian (the font, tower screen and pulpit by Ferrey, the reredos by G. E. Street, as is much of the stained glass. The finest window is the Last Judgement window in the tower by Alexander Gibbs, 1862. There are a lot of memorial tablets on the walls, but the best monument is in the outer north aisle where Robert Gray (d. 1638) stands life-sized and colourful under a rounded pediment flanked by Ionic columns. The inscription below is well worth reading. He founded the almshouses in East Street in 1635.

41. TRULL, ALL SAINTS

Trull has been absorbed by the spread of Taunton but the area around the church still has a village-like feel. The exterior of the church is rather plain with a thirteenth-century west tower. The rest is fifteenth century with nave and aisles with porches and chancel with vestry to the north. The south aisle and porch have battlements, the north side does not and the porch is quite humble here. The simple interior has only a beam where you would expect a chancel arch but it is not the architecture that draws people here but the splendid woodwork and medieval stained glass. The east window has a fine Crucifixion scene with Christ on the cross flanked by the Virgin Mary and St John. In the tracery above are the four symbols of the Evangelists. There is a collection of bench ends from the mid-sixteenth century with varied designs including the Instruments of the Passion and individuals originally forming part of a procession but now dispersed among the benches. It was led by a boy carrying a large cross. Foliage, tracery and profiles are other designs. The chancel and chapels are separated from the nave and aisles by medieval screens, those to the chapels light and airy with four-light

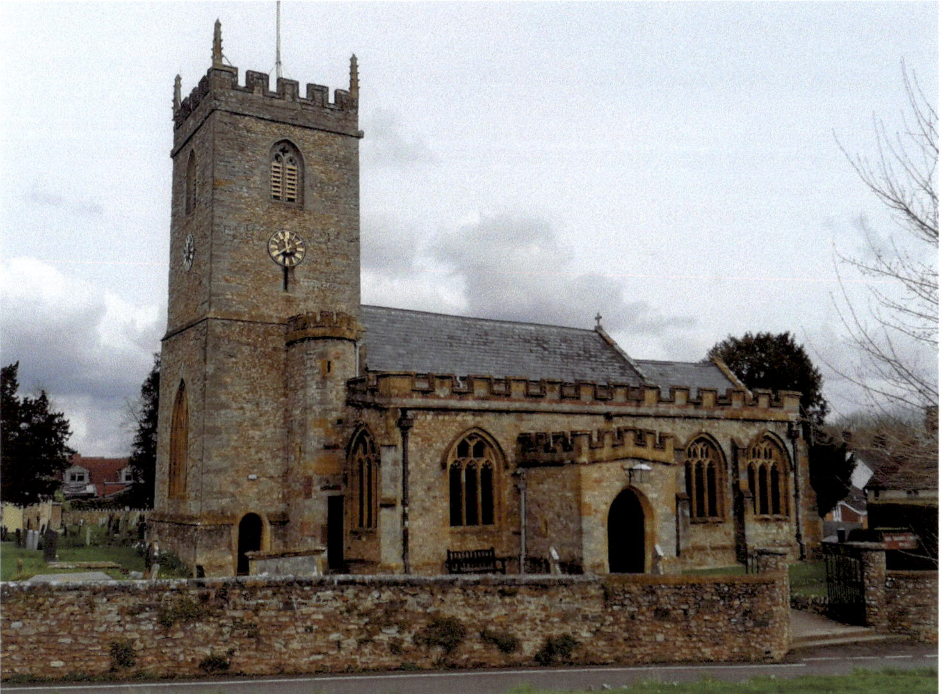

Trull. The exterior from the south.

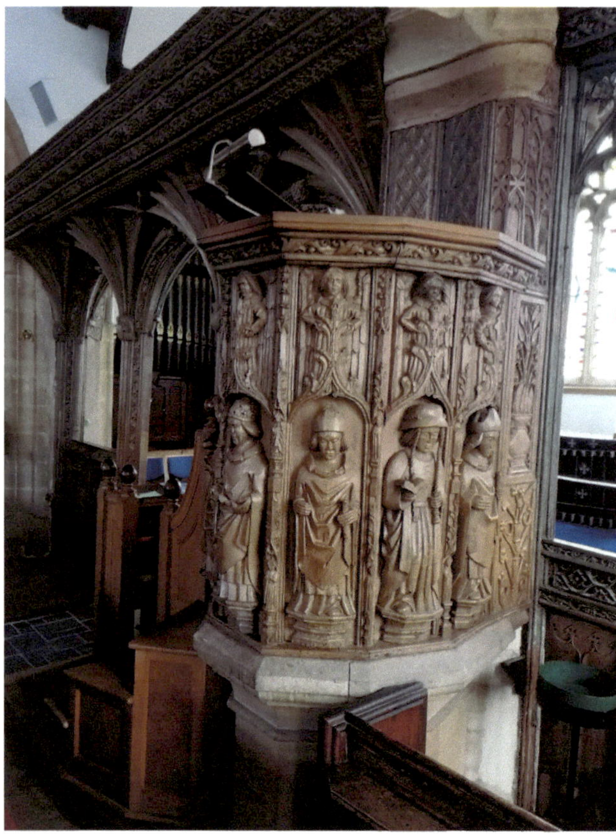

Trull. The precious pulpit with the unrestored figures of the Four Doctors of the Church, plus St John the Evangelist.

traceried openings. The rood screen survives but without its loft and minus any tracery in the large openings, but the coving and cresting are very fine and the rear has painted decoration which was probably done in the eighteenth century. The panels below the openings are also painted but with foliage designs and some faces. However, the most precious survival is the marvellous pulpit with its original and undefaced statues of St John the Evangelist and four Doctors of the church, Ambrose, Jerome, Augustine, and Pope Gregory the Great. The canopies above the figures are held up by angels.

42. WATCHET, ST DECUMAN

The parish church at Watchet is not in the centre or by the harbour but outside of the town on the hill above, an area now known as St Decumans. St Decuman was a Christian hermit from Pembrokeshire and legend says he crossed the sea on a raft with a cow. He settled on the cliffs near what is today Daw's castle. A local man decapitated him, whereafter he picked up his head, washed it in a holy well and replaced it. His death is recorded as around 706, whether from decapitation or old age is not known. A minster grew up around his hermitage, as did a Saxon settlement, but both were affected by coastal erosion and Viking

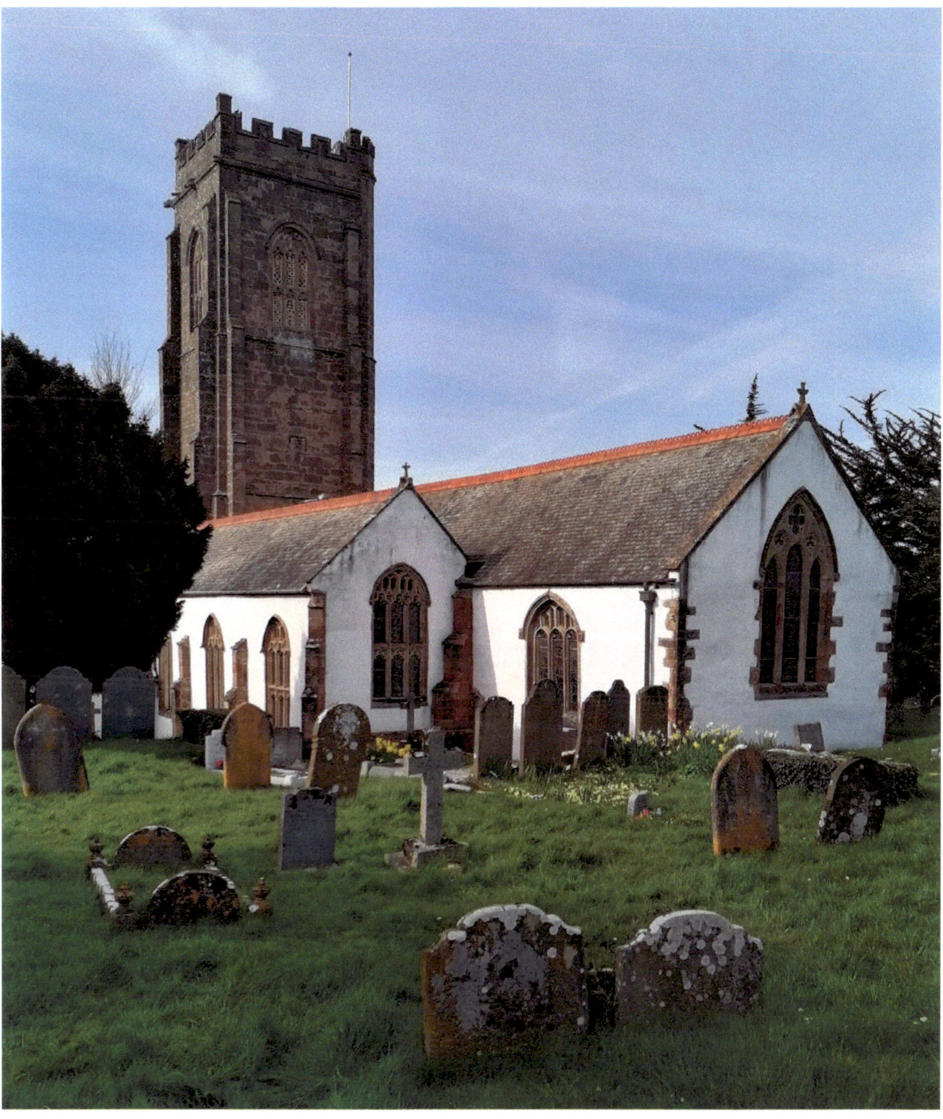

Watchet. The church, seen from the south-east, stands in a large churchyard.

raids. Eventually the original site was abandoned and the new church built, and the bones of St Decuman were moved to the present church. The town itself was rebuilt to the east. The oldest part of the church is the thirteenth-century chancel – see the north lancet and the east window of three stepped lights with two trefoils and a quatrefoil above. The rest of the church was rebuilt in the late fifteenth century and the first years of the sixteenth century. It has a tall tower, similar to that at Minehead and Winsford, nave and aisles with south porch and a projecting chancel, its roof continuous with that of the nave. The south side is plainer than the north and whitened like the chancel. However, the east bay has transomed

Perpendicular windows as found at Selworthy and nearby Cleeve Abbey. The north side is much showier built of squared blocks of sandstone, and with an embattled parapet and projecting taller rood stair turret. The windows here are four-centred and the merlons (the upright projections of the battlements) have quatrefoils. The interior is remarkably unified, but closer observation reveals subtle differences. The arcades are four bays long with a wider fifth bay of the same height beyond the rather apologetic chancel arch. The pillars of the north arcade have shallow niches, two have original statues. There are wagon roofs throughout with bosses and carved wall plates, the latter with foliage trails between shield-carrying angels. There are three screens of *c.* 1500, all much restored, the rood screen with four-light divisions, and two screens to the south chapel, that to the west with six-light divisions with thick central mullion and the parclose screen with three-light divisions, the lights with pretty traceried heads. The chancel has medieval tiles between the stalls and these date from the thirteenth century. There are also some notable monuments and brasses, mainly in the north or Wyndham chapel. Of particular note are the two upright black marble slabs on the east wall, on the right Sir John Wyndham (d. 1572) and Florence Wadham his wife (d. 1596), with large figures and enamelled heraldry, and to the left Sir John (d. 1645), their son, and wife Joanna with highly unusual square brass relief portraits. The hanging monument with two kneeling figures commemorates two of the latter's sons Henry (d. 1613) and George (d. 1624) and the splendid baroque monument between is that of his grandson Sir William (d. 1683). The ensuing Wyndham

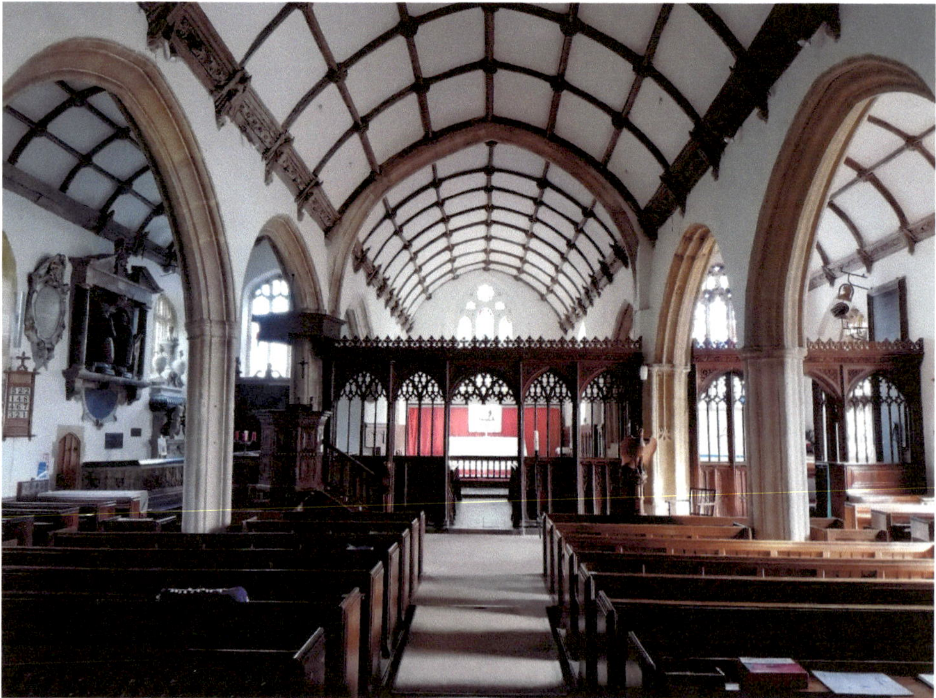

Watchet. The fine interior with wagon roofs which have much rich detailing.

dynasty almost didn't happen as it was thought his pregnant mother Florence had died and she was laid to rest in a coffin in the Wyndham chapel. She revived when a sexton tried to cut off a finger to steal her rings. She walked back home to the grieving, then astonished family and it is said to this day that no Wyndham is buried until three days after their death.

No trace remains of St Decuman's shrine (or the original minster) but St Decuman's Holy Well is to the north of the church in the woods (and signposted from the road).

43. WEDMORE, ST MARY

This large church is on a rise above the village centre. It is mainly fourteenth- and fifteenth-century Perpendicular, cruciform, with a tall central tower and a fine three-storeyed south porch. Some earlier features do remain, most notably the very fine Early English south doorway (with door dated 1677), the crossing of a similar date, and a fine cusped east window in the south chancel chapel. On my last few visits here, the entrance from the porch is via a second smaller doorway into the outer south chapel built in the angle between the porch and the south transept. Despite the absence of a clerestory, the interior is surprisingly light and airy, thanks to the large side windows, and the very slim five-bayed arcades. Three large candelabra hang in the nave, the oldest of 1779, the others 1856. On the pillar behind the ornate Jacobean pulpit is a large wall painting of

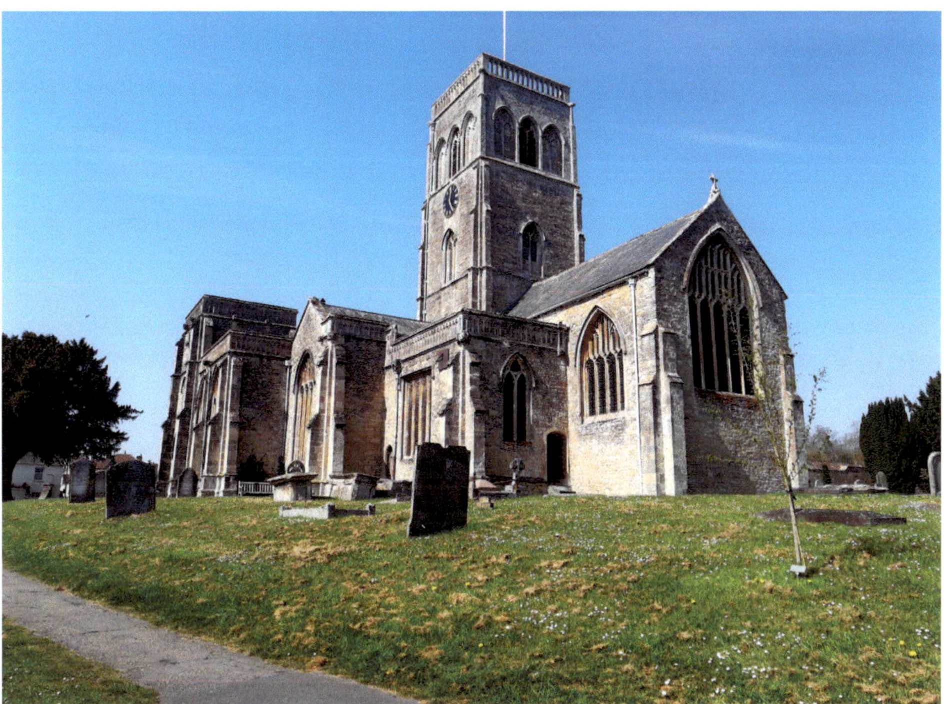

Wedmore. This fine church is grouped around its tall central tower.

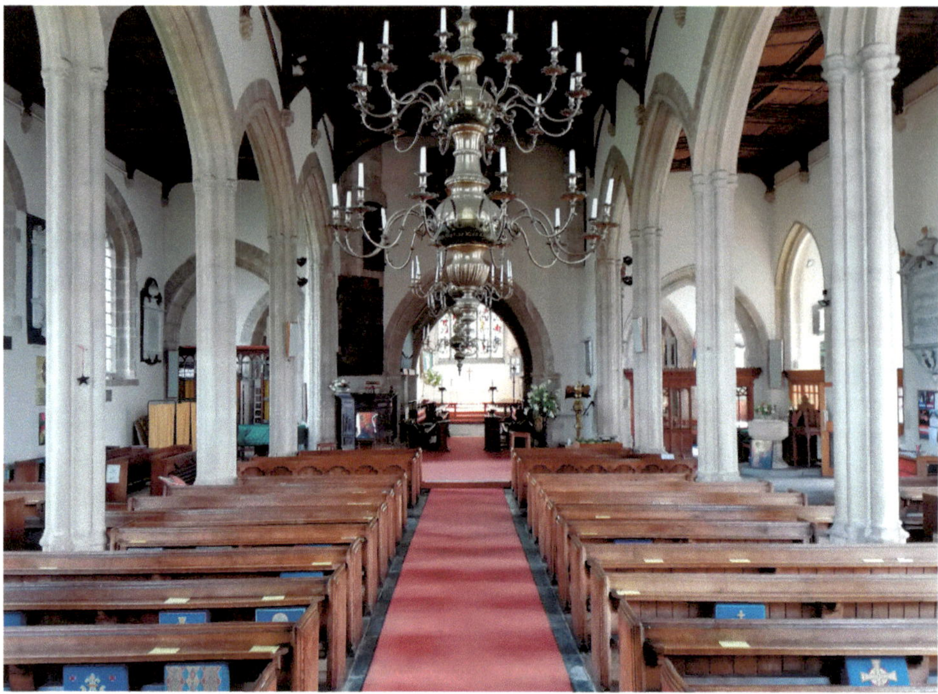

Wedmore. The spacious interior looking east.

St Christopher, the head of the Child Jesus mid-fifteenth century, surviving from an overpainting of *c.* 1520; note the mermaid and ships around the feet of the saint. There are two memorial brasses in the vestry (north chapel), one to a man who died at the siege of Antwerp in 1585, the body buried there but the heart returned to Wedmore, and the other a rather jaunty figure dressed as a cavalier (d. 1634). The east and west windows are by Clayton & Bell (1888 and 1890, respectively), the latter, unusually, with panels showing King Alfred burning the cakes and the Royal Court with Queen Victoria. Somewhere near Wedmore Alfred had a palace and after he had defeated the Danes at Edington in 878, the Danish king Guthrum came to Wedmore to sign a peace treat known as the Treaty of Wedmore.

44. WELLS, ST CUTHBERT

Somerset's largest parish church, it is sometimes mistaken by visitors arriving at the coach station for the cathedral. It also had a starring role in the 2007 film *Hot Fuzz* along with other places in the city. The church was built for the townspeople and was the civic church for the mayor and corporation. The church consists of a proud west tower, nave and crossing in one, aisles with south porch and opposite a treasury on the north and east of these projections two-bayed outer aisles and transepts, and chancel with north and south chapels. Externally nearly everything is fifteenth-century Perpendicular, except for the east window of the south transept, the windows of the treasury, and the fine sixteenth-century clerestory. The porch is vaulted but shelters a doorway of *c.* 1300. On entering the church, it becomes obvious that the church is older. It must have been a similar size in the thirteenth century, ingeniously enlarged in the early fifteenth century when the arcades were increased in height by the raising of the pillars with higher bases. The west bay is fifteenth century, built when the tower was constructed. The clerestory and roof are sixteenth century, a fine addition but clearly so as the fifteenth-century roof gable appears over the tower arch. The roof was repainted in 1963. The crossing arches are separated from the nave arcades by a short piece of wall with a small opening, the clerestory and roof continuing above. The east crossing arch to the chancel remains with window above but the western arch was taken down at the time the former central tower was removed in 1561 following its collapse. The church must have looked impressive with both a central and

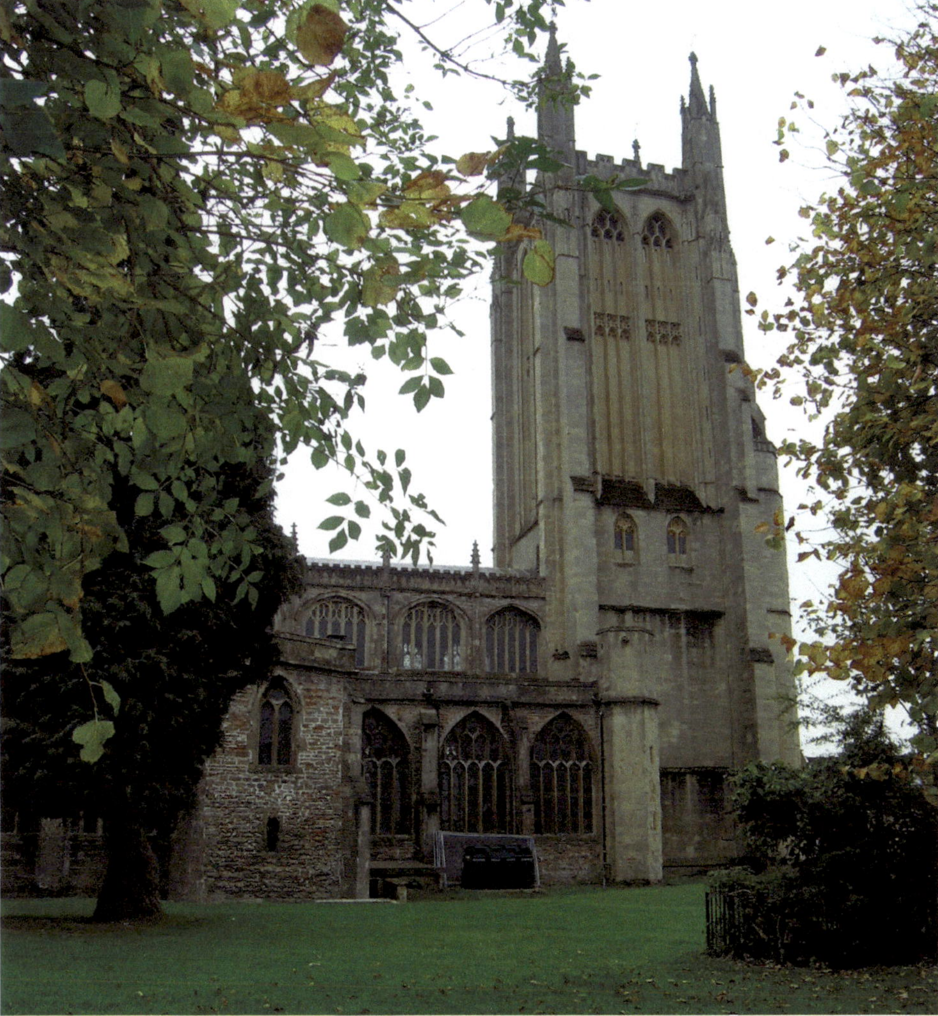

Wells, St Cuthbert. The fine tower of Somerset's largest parish church.

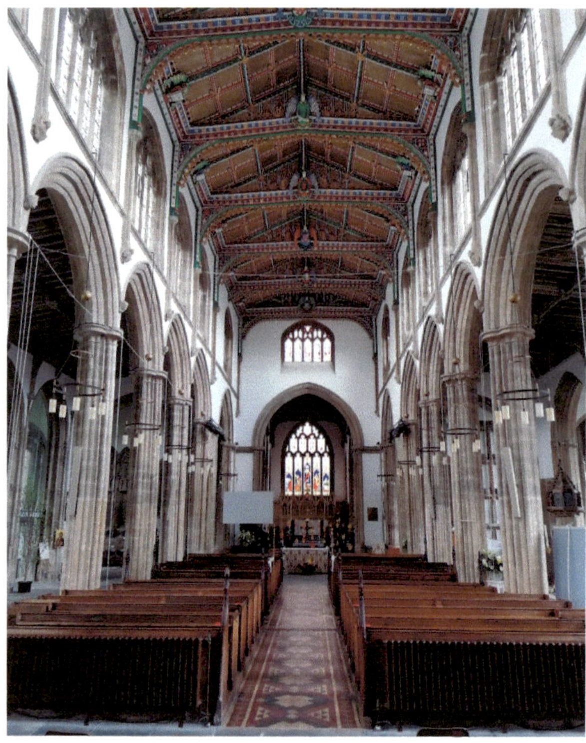

Wells, St Cuthbert. The interior showing the fine roof that was repainted in 1963.

west tower. The east walls of both transepts have remains of large reredoses, the details hacked away after the Reformation and both plastered over; they were only rediscovered in 1848. That in the south transept was based on the Tree of Jesse and the figure of Jesse is clearly identifiable. Among the fittings, there are two royal arms (Charles I and Charles II), and a busily carved pulpit dated 1636 with naïve panels of scenes from the Old Testament. There is also a wall memorial to Henry Keillinghusen (d. 1615) with the inscription: 'borne in Hamburghe in Germanye who came to see this countrye and learne the language'.

The other church in the city, St Thomas, 1856–57 by S. S. Teulon, made world news in February 2022 when the top of its spire was blown down during Storm Eunice, an event captured on video by a local teenager.

45. WESTONZOYLAND, ST MARY THE VIRGIN

The earliest part of this church is the chancel – see the two Decorated side windows on each side – but otherwise the church is a complete rebuilding of *c.* 1500 using blue lias with stone dressings. Construction unusually seems to have begun with the splendid tower, a landmark rising above the Levels and a witness to the Battle of Sedgemoor in 1685. It is over 100 feet tall (30m) and inside has a fan vault. The nave, aisles, south transept and south porch are all embattled, the smaller north porch, north transept and chancel have plain parapets. The interior is wide light and spacious, the nave with arcades to the aisles of five bays and taller wider sixth bay into the transepts. Above the nave is one of the grand wooden roofs of Somerset, a feat of medieval carpentry. The wall plates and tie beams are topped with pierced cresting; in the centre of the sides of each bay winged angels and the tie beam also has similar angels on each side above a central boss, which carries a king post with tracery panels each side to the apex of the roof. Many benches have traceried ends of *c.* 1500 but the organ case, rood screen and loft, the rood figures

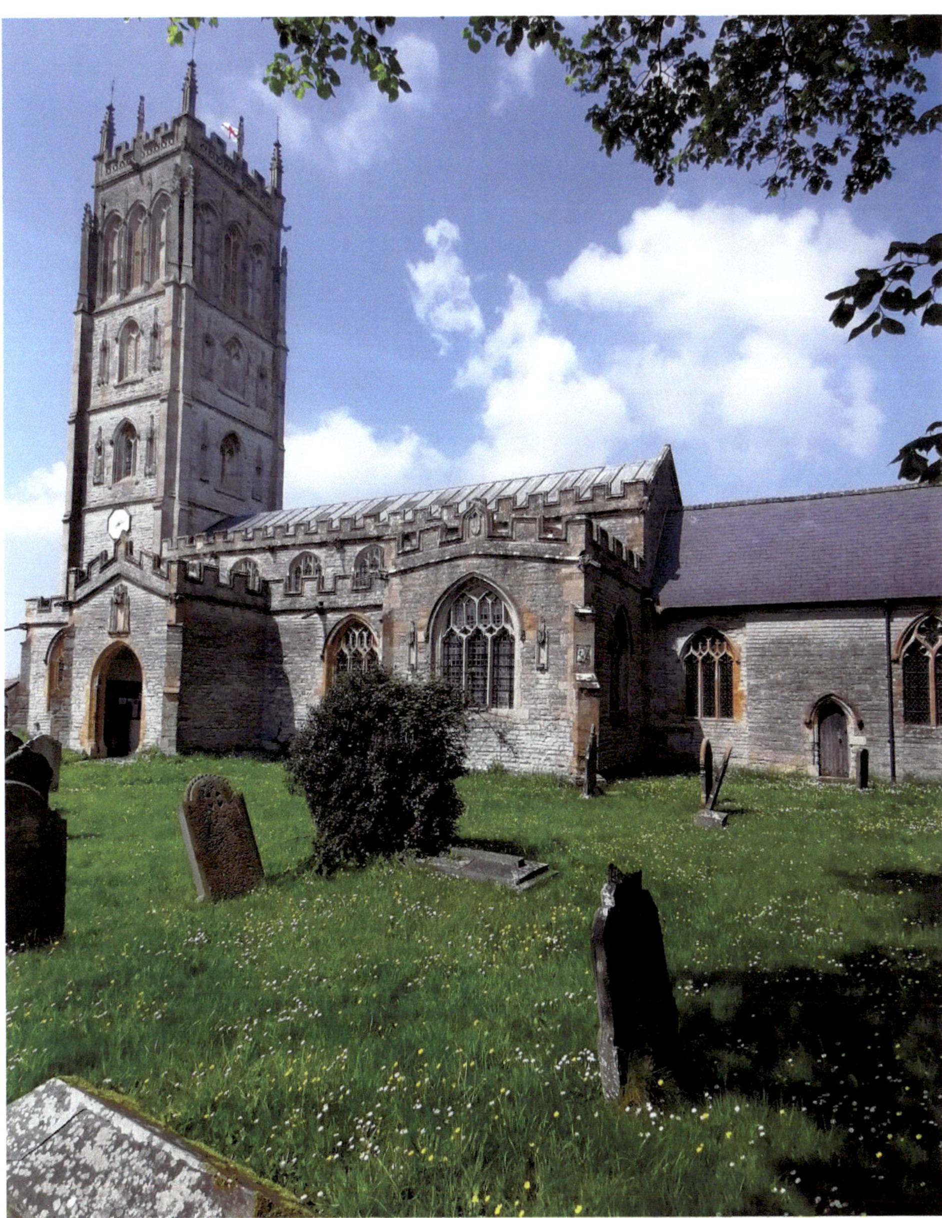

Westonzoyland. This fine church is situated close to the site of the Battle of Sedgemoor.

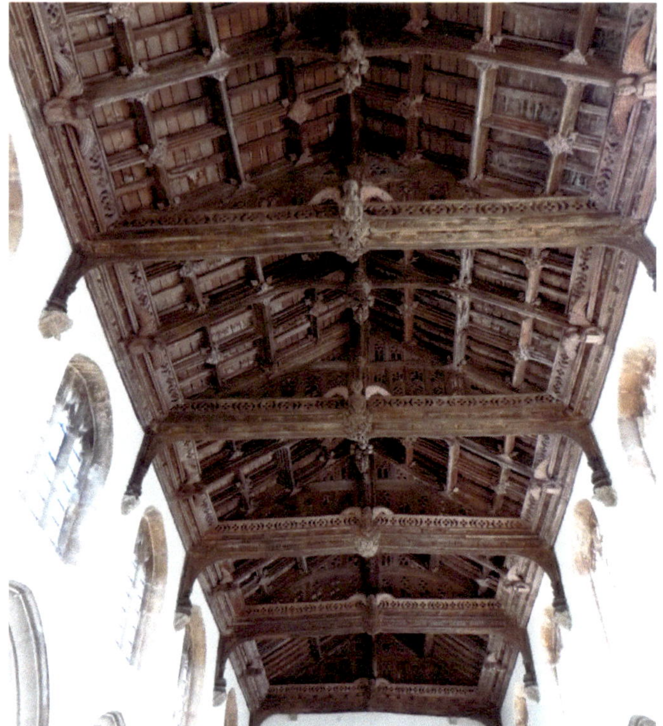

Westonzoyland. The nave
has another very fine
roof, which is typical in
Somerset.

and the choir fittings were installed by W. D. Caroë, 1935–36. Under a recess in
the north transept lies an effigy of a priest praying. The west end of the south aisle
has an interesting museum area with artefacts, manikins and audio-visual displays
charting the history of the Monmouth Rebellion and the Battle of Sedgemoor.
Following the battle many of the injured rebels were locked up in the church and
entries in the church registers record how money had to be spent on frankincense
to make God's house sweet again.

46. WINSCOMBE, ST JAMES THE GREAT

The church is situated on a hillside and well away from the large village in the valley
below. It has a car park to the east of the church and you have to pass through some
remarkable metal gates installed in 2012 to commemorate the diamond jubilee of
Queen Elizabeth II. The divisions are all irregular in shape and several finish in
heads of lilies. The tall tower, 100 feet (30m) high, dates from around 1400, of four
stages with two-light windows to each stage; the top stage window is flanked by
two blank similar windows. It resembles several other towers, especially Banwell,
and the second stage above the west window had like Banwell an Annunciation
scene; the lily vase survives but the two niches alongside are now empty. Both aisles
are a little later than the tower, that on the north with a parapet matching that of
the tower (as does the north porch) and with a restored medieval roof. The tower
has a busy lierne vault. The nave roof, with two tiers of angels, dates from John

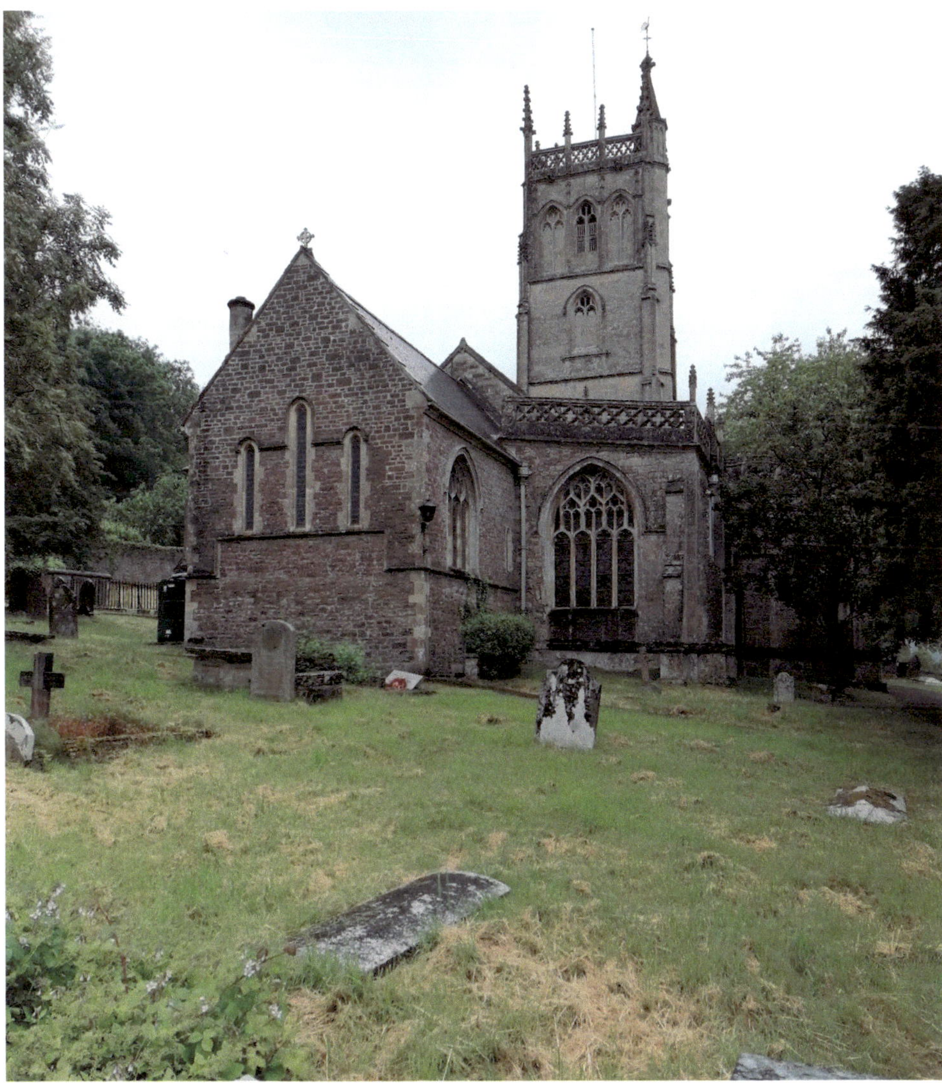

Winscombe. The view from the east approaching from the car park.

Norton's restoration of 1863. He rebuilt the chancel, inspired by Early English details found during demolition of the old chancel but one of the lancets could be original thirteenth-century work. The glass in the east window is by William Burges. The main interest here is the medieval stained glass in the north chapel, south aisle and chancel windows. William Warrington collected glass from other windows in 1850 to create the east window of the north aisle; it has a beautiful Crucifixion scene and also below four pairs of kneeling donors, each man with a purse and each woman with a rosary. The Virgin has a red mantle and to her left completing the window is St Anthony with a pig at his feet. In the same aisle is an incomplete figure of the Virgin flanked by St Catherine (left) and St John the

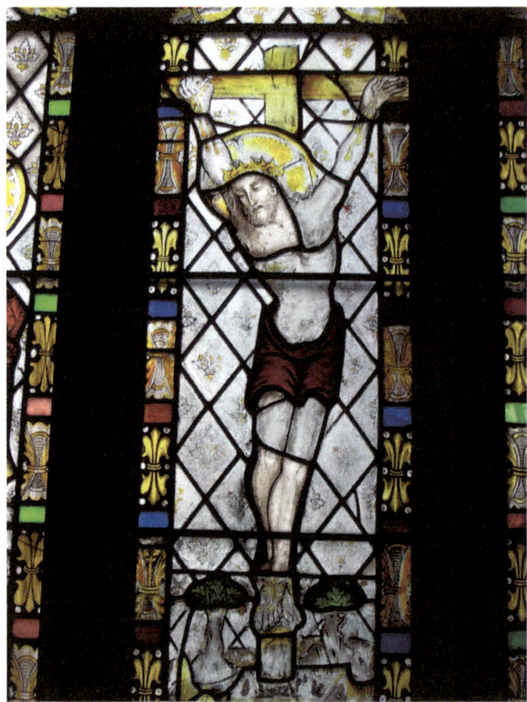

Winscombe. Medieval glass of the Crucifixion in the east window of the north aisle.

Baptist (right). In the chancel a window has three St Peters, each holding a book, and St Peter the Deacon holds a cross, St Peter the Apostle holds keys, and St Peter the Exorcist holds a gold holy water sprinkler. In the south aisle is a window with St James flanked by a bishop (left) and an archbishop (right).

47. WITHAM FRIARY, BLESSED VIRGIN MARY, ST JOHN THE BAPTIST AND ALL SAINTS

A lengthy dedication for a small but very important church, part of the first Carthusian foundation (*c.* 1178) in the country which was one of three monasteries established by Henry II in expiation for the murder of Thomas Becket. Hugh of Avalon (St Hugh of Lincoln) became prior in 1179 and this church, a mile or so to the west of the priory, was probably built to serve the lay brothers and, later, the village that had grown up around the priory. An earlier church had been built here in around 1140 by Bruton Priory and the walls of this building were strengthened to take a stone vault. Originally three bays with an apse, a fourth bay with a steep bellcote was added to the west by William White in 1876, replacing a tower of 1828. The flying buttresses are also White's. On stepping inside, it is like being in a village church in Normandy, stone vaulting being uncommon in small churches in England. The round-headed side windows have fragments of medieval glass on the north and the four south windows have scenes from the life of St Hugh by Comper. The cresting from the fifteenth-century rood screen adorns the top of the Jacobean pulpit, giving it a rather strange appearance.

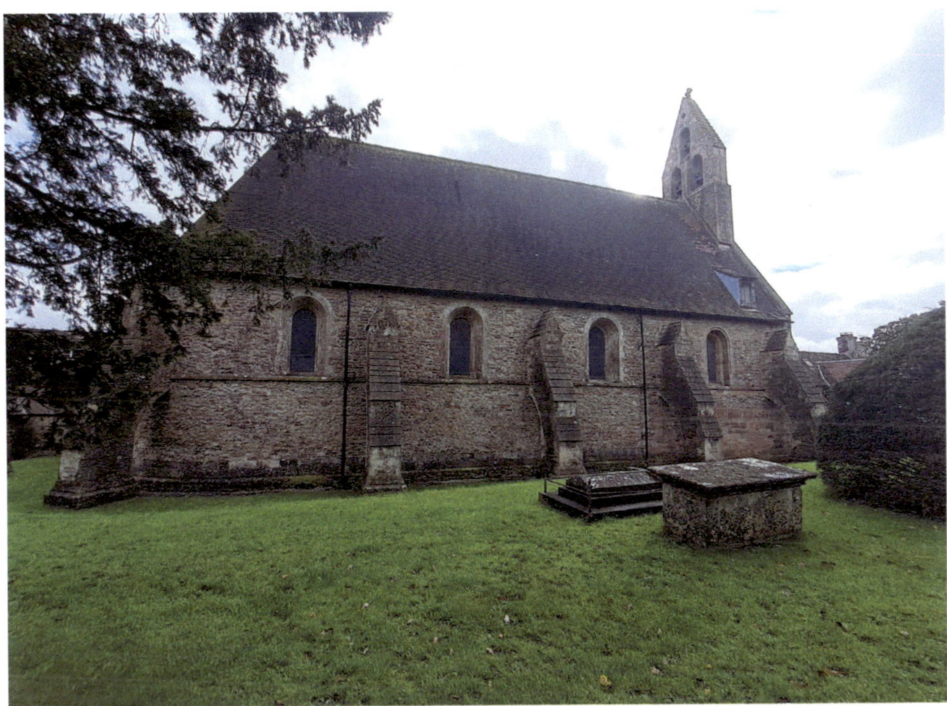

Above: Witham Friary.
View from the north.

Right: Witham Friary. The
interior is reminiscent of French
village churches.

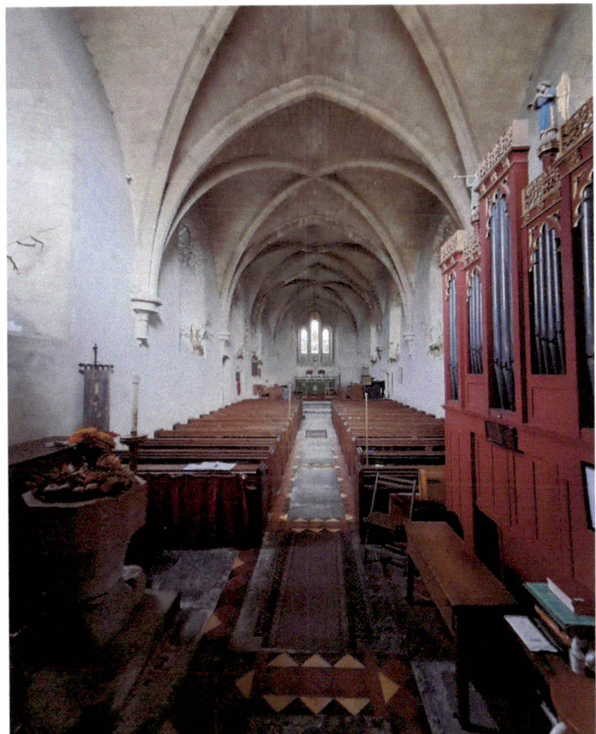

48. WYKE CHAMPFLOWER, HOLY TRINITY

This unexpected little gem was built in 1623–24 by Henry Southworth, the former date on the outer doorway of the porch and the latter on the tympanum inside marking the division between nave and chancel. It stands behind the manor house to which it is attached and the room over the porch is in fact part of the house and a bathroom! Peeping over the house as you approach the church is an exquisite bell turret, a tower in miniature with its embattled parapet and angle pinnacles. Inside is a complete set of original furnishings including box pews with acorn finials and panelling with hat pegs, font cover (the font itself dates from 1945) and an overlarge stone pulpit with strapwork pilasters and bands of foliage. The large tympanum divides nave and sanctuary and has three coats of arms: in the centre the royal arms of James I; to the left Archbishop George, Abbot of Canterbury; and to the right Arthur Lake, Bishop of Bath & Wells, who consecrated the church in 1624. The rear of the tympanum was painted over in the early twentieth century and the two shields and scriptural texts were lost. In the chancel is the hanging monument to Henry who died a year after completion of his church in 1625. When Henry bought the manor in 1608, he found the church to be in 'great ruine and decay' so he pulled it down and rebuilt anew, extending the church by 20 feet (60m). This predecessor may have been little more than a private chapel, built somewhere between 1135 and 1154 for Luke de Champflower and given to the canons of Bruton Abbey who undertook to maintain it and say mass here

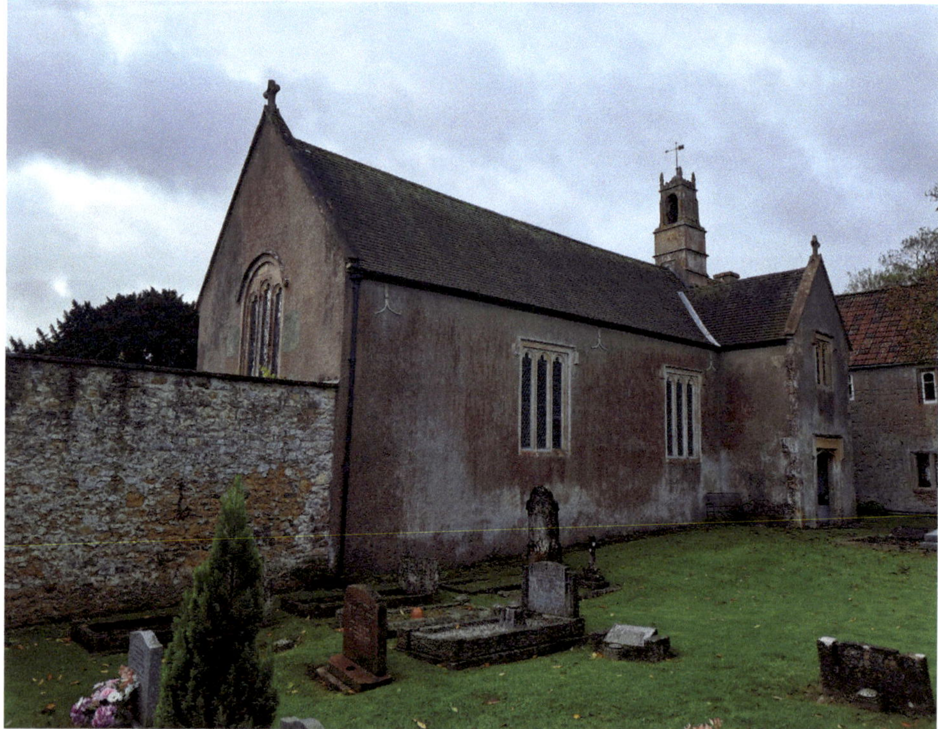

Wyke Champflower. From the north-east. The church adjoins the manor house.

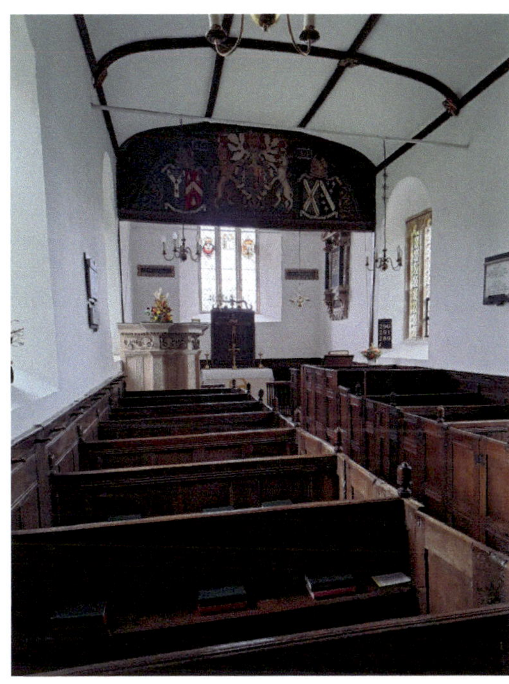

Wyke Champflower. The charming
interior of 1624.

every Monday and on feast days. The neglect of the chapel may have followed the
Dissolution of the abbey.

There is a similar earlier arrangement of a church attached to a manor house at
nearby Lytes Cary, now belonging to the National Trust.

49. YATTON, ST MARY THE VIRGIN

The odd appearance of this church from afar is due to the missing top of the spire,
truncated in 1595. It must have been a splendid sight above the moors. From
the outside the church appears mainly Perpendicular of the mid-fifteenth century
but this work is in fact a remodelling of an earlier building. The low thirteenth-
century crossing and base of the central tower are the oldest parts although here
too the arches have been altered to match the work in the nave where aisles were
added and the nave heightened with a clerestory. The fine wagon roof in the nave
has carved bosses and angels on the wall plate. The chancel was altered at the
same time and a vault was inserted into the crossing. The tripartite west front,
with turrets flanking the six-light west window and smaller ones to the aisles,
has only two other parallels in England's parish churches, at Crewkerne (q.v.)
and St Mary at Beverley, in the East Riding of Yorkshire. The handsome vaulted
south porch is late fifteenth century as is the north-east chapel. The transepts are
early fourteenth-century Decorated work. See the south window with intersecting
tracery and the ogee headed tomb recesses under the north window. These recesses
contain effigies of a civilian and his wife (*c.* 1325). Freestanding in the transept is
the fine alabaster monument to Sir Richard Newton (d. 1449) and wife (d. 1475).

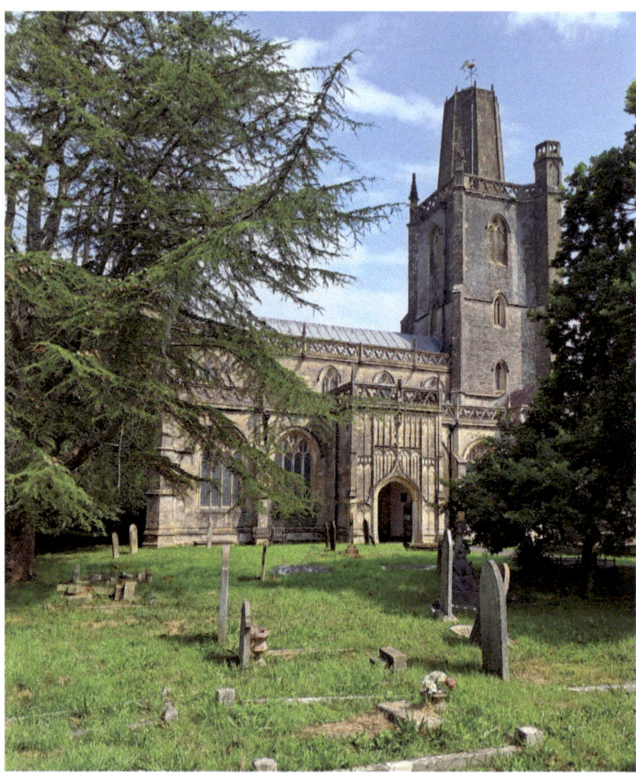

Left: Yatton. The truncated spire is quite a local landmark.

Below left: Yatton. The stately interior.

Below right: Yatton. Monuments in the north chapel.

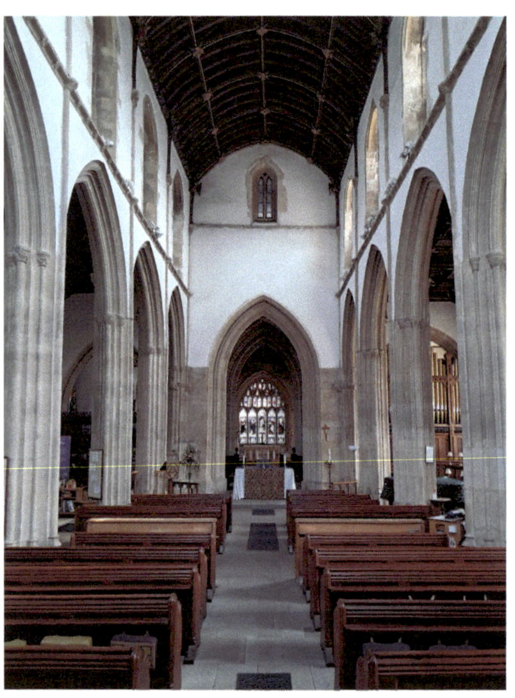

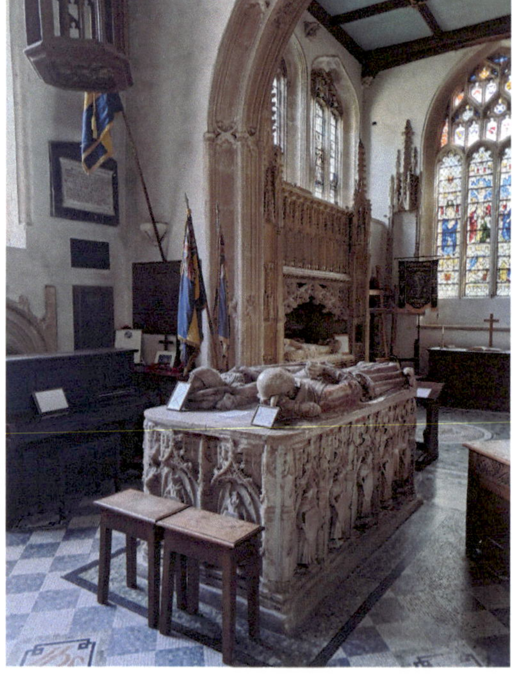

Their finely detailed effigies lie on top of a tomb chest decorated with shield-carrying angels in ogee-headed niches. In the north chapel is the monument to Sir John Newton (d. 1488) and his wife Isobel (d. 1498); their recessed effigies lie on a tomb chest decorated with quatrefoils. On the wall behind them is a relief of the Annunciation, with a dove coming down from Heaven and looking like a jet aircraft with vapour trails behind it! The Tudor arch and its pierced spandrels are decorated with a profusion of crockets and, above, a row of ten (now empty) niches. At the west end of the nave are the life-size figures of St Peter and St Paul which were part of an organ case at Bath Abbey. To the north of the church is an octagonal meeting room built in 1975 and connected to the north aisle by a glazed passage. It is worth walking down here to admire the ornate north doorway and to purchase from a range of excellent sweet and savoury preserves on sale here.

50. YEOVIL, ST JOHN THE BAPTIST

The church was entirely rebuilt in the later fourteenth century and is remarkable for its large windows, more glass than walls, earning it the tag of 'The Lantern of the West'. Remains of an earlier church which stood next to the tower were removed in 1854–55 and portions reconstructed in The Chantry, now outside the churchyard to the west. The new church, completed by 1400, consists of the west tower, a nave and aisles of five bays with the last bay extended north and south as transepts, a south porch and chancel of three bays with two-bayed side chapels. The fall of the ground at the east end enabled a crypt to be built. The organ chamber and lower vestries on the north side were added in the 1890s and 1914, respectively. The tower is of four stages with set back buttresses and a

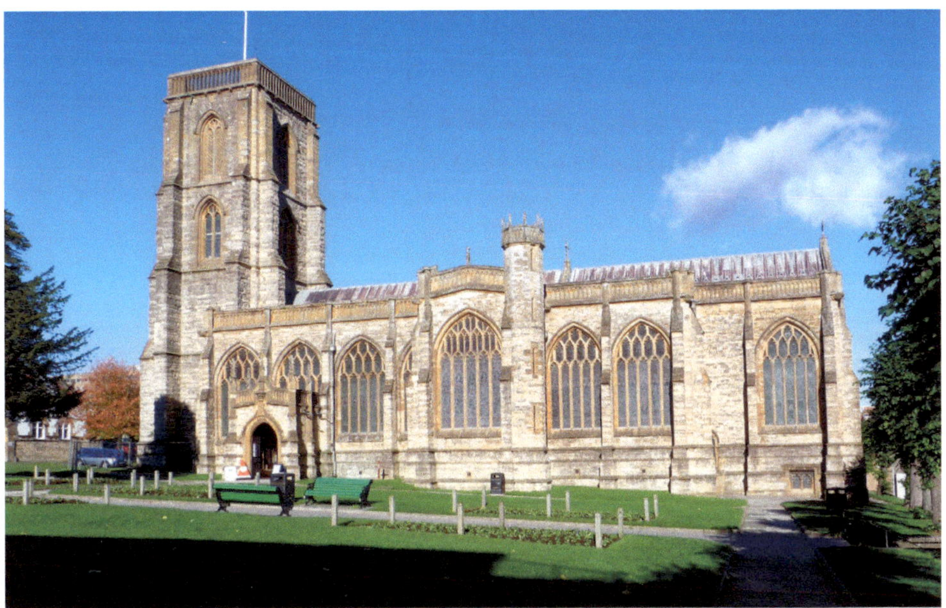

Yeovil, St John the Baptist. The large aisle windows of 'the Lantern of the West'.

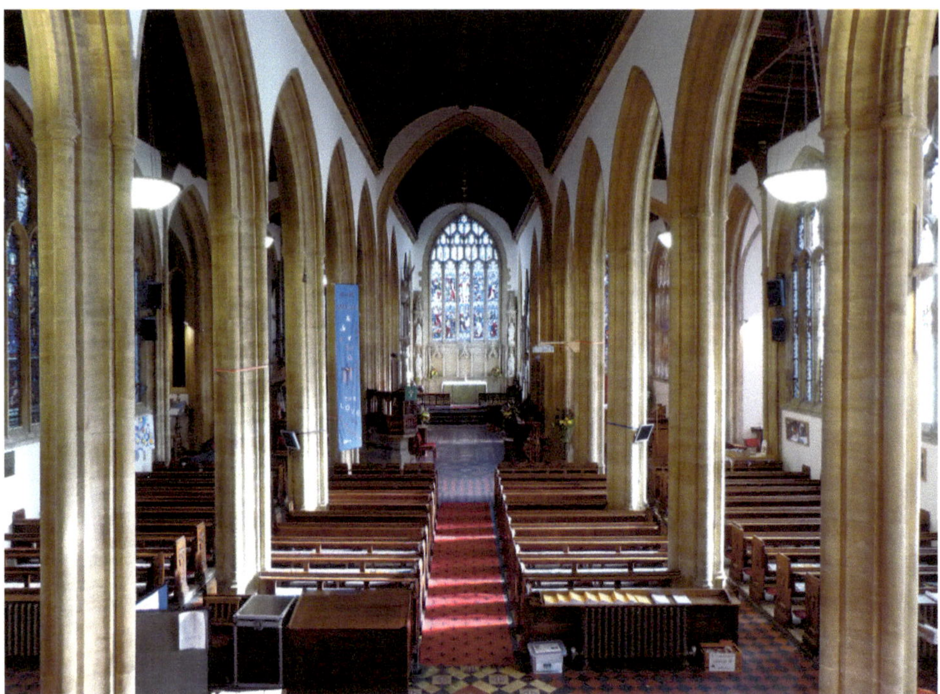

Yeovil, St John the Baptist. The interior from the ringing chamber.

parapet of close-set arcading which is blank in the corners. Similar blank parapets to the south side of the church, those on the north are plain. The transepts have an octagonal stair turret in the outer eastern angles. The interior is lofty and light, a continual space interrupted only by the chancel arch and arches into the side chapels. There is no clerestory, but the large side windows flood the interior with light. The two large head corbels in the chancel once carried the Lenten Veil. There is an ornate doorway to the stairs leading to the crypt; note the miniature rib vault with bosses inside. The crypt itself is square with a central column to support the vaulting. There are a large number of wall memorials, including a pair of brass figures now removed from their original position in the chancel floor where the original stone has been inscribed to that effect! The best of the eighteenth-century monuments is that to the Harbin family (1711) in the north transept. There are also several good stained-glass windows, the best by Henry Holiday (1917) in the north aisle, a memorial to two brothers, Charles and Cecil Prowse, killed during the First World War. However, the most prized position is the medieval brass lectern, sadly now confined to the north transept. It was made on the Continent in around 1450 and has an inscription and depiction of the donor on the shelf, Frater Martinus Forester, a monk. The lectern was purchased in London in 1541 and the parish paid *2d* in 1565 'for the puttinge owt of the two pictors upon the brass dexte that the lessuns be read on' when the face of the monk was erased. Finally, the churchyard is usually well planted with flowers and shrubs and is a little oasis of peace in the busy town centre shopping area.